Songs of Two Homelands

Hymns and Liturgy
of the
Augustana Lutheran Tradition

edited by
Ronald T. Englund
Glenn C. Stone
John O. Swanson

Augustana Heritage Association
Chicago, Illinois

The cover design is adapted from *Hemlandssånger* (Songs of the Homeland)
published in 1892 by the Evangelical Lutheran Augustana Synod

First published - 2000
Songs of Two Homelands: Hymns and Liturgy of the Augustana Lutheran Tradition
Augustana Heritage Association, 1100 East 55th Street, Chicago, IL 60615-5199
Introduction and new material © 2000 by Augustana Heritage Association

Library of Congress Card Number: 00-105322
ISBN: 0-9676573-1-8

Printed and bound in the United States of America
by Cape Cod Printing Inc., A Carlson Company
Falmouth, Massachusetts

Songs of Two Homelands

We are grateful to
Aid Association for Lutherans
for generous support
in publishing this book

AID ASSOCIATION FOR LUTHERANS

Table of Contents

Introduction

Hemlandet, Det Gamla och det Nya (Homeland, The Old and the New) was the title the pioneer leaders of the emerging Swedish Lutheran community in North America gave the newspaper they founded in 1855. When this journal became primarily political in content, it was supplemented by another publication, *Det Ratta Hemlandet* (The True Homeland), devoted exclusively to religion. Both titles pointed to dual concerns of those who were in 1860 to found the Swedish Evangelical Lutheran Augustana Synod. On the one hand, they reflected the ties both to Sweden, the old homeland of their birth, and to America, the new homeland of their adoption; on the other hand, they focused on the obligations of earthly citizenship which their immigrant experience impressed upon them, and the "citizenship in heaven" which was the ultimate goal of their pilgrimage.

To guide their worship life, Augustana congregations from the beginning used an 1849 revision of the 1819 *Psalmbok* of the Church of Sweden; by 1865 a North American edition was available. In 1860 a Swedish-American supplement, *Hemlandssånger* (Songs of the Homeland) had been privately published. Three decades later, under the same title, again invoking the "homeland" imagery, this became an official Synod book. In issuing the present collection to help perpetuate "the Augustana tradition in hymnody and liturgy," the editors thought it appropriate to turn once again to that historic theme. So here we present *Songs of Two Homelands*. The implication again is multi-dimensional: horizontally - songs from Sweden and America; vertically - the earthly music which echoes the heavenly psalms of "the True Homeland."

To distill that rich heritage into a book of [146] pages is a daunting task indeed. For most of those who remember the Augustana Evangelical Lutheran Church almost 40 years after it was melded into a larger body, the centerpiece of the Augustana heritage is *The Hymnal and Order of Service* (1925), a collection of 680 hymns and more than 300 pages of liturgical texts. But at least seven other sources published during the Augustana Church's 102 years of corporate life were also consulted in preparing this volume.

Besides *Hemlandssånger* (1892), these include the *Koral-Bok* (1884); *Hymnal and Order of Service* (1899); *Hymnal and Order of Service* (1901); *Söndagsskolbok* (Sunday School Book) (1903); *Lutherförbundets Sångbok* (Luther League Song Book) (*1913*); and *The Junior Hymnal* (1928).

Obviously, to produce a coherent and useful collection, selection had to be guided by strict criteria. The editors recognize that in any such process personal taste cannot be avoided. We know too that Augustana was a large enough church geographically and culturally that regional and generational differences in understanding the "heritage" also come into play. We have tried to produce a collection of hymns distinctive of the total heritage, to help new generations appreciate some of the best that Swedish/Augustana worship has to offer. At the same time we have tried to produce a book that can be used as a supplement in both parish and special settings today when there is a desire to explore the heritage anew. That said, users of this book deserve to know the criteria which helped the editors make the decisions which resulted in *Songs of Two Homelands*.

First, we looked for hymnody that would be representative of the best known and historically most important hymns, in text and/or music, which Augustana inherited from the Church of Sweden. These range from chorales of the Reformation period through songs of the 19th century awakening movements.

Second, we looked for hymns written in America by Augustana Lutherans: such authors as E.E. Ryden, Ernst W. Olson and Samuel M. Miller.

Third, we tried to include a fair sampling of hymns from the wider German, English and American traditions, which were in the Augustana Hymnal, were much beloved in the Augustana Church, and are not found in the currently used worship books of the Evangelical Lutheran Church in America. The presumption is that this book will most often be used in settings where current hymn books are available, so that it is unnecessary to duplicate certain hymns, popular in Augustana congregations, that remain readily accessible today.

Fourth, there are some hymns so prominent in Augustana usage that their presence is demanded in an "Augustana heritage" collection even though they remain available in current hymn books, albeit at times in different translations.

Fifth, we tried to produce a collection which would include music for the various seasons of the Church Year, and would relate to a wide spectrum of themes in terms of doctrine and piety.

The choice of liturgy was much easier. The historic Swedish High Mass, first in the mother tongue and then in English translation, was the standard for most Augustana churches. It is reproduced here in a form that combines The Service (without Communion) with The Holy Communion with Full Service, so that all the major elements of the liturgy and its music are available.

It should be remembered that during the last five years of its separate life, the Augustana Church's official worship book was the 1958 *Service Book and Hymnal* (SBH). The Second Setting of the liturgy in that volume was a major Augustana contribution to the wider heritage of Lutheran worship in North America. Regina Fryxell's liturgical music, largely based on Swedish and other continental sources, eventually proved to be the SBH's most popular setting.

Finally, we would echo the words with which our sainted predecessors who compiled the Hymnal of 1925 concluded their Preface: if this book "can serve, in some small degree, the purpose of the Lord Jesus Christ, for love of Whom we have labored, the Committee will feel abundantly satisfied."

Ronald T. Englund, Glenn C. Stone, John O. Swanson

Prepare the Way, O Zion!

Bereden väg för Herran. 7 6, 7 6, 7 7, 6 6. Old Swedish Melody, prior to 1560.

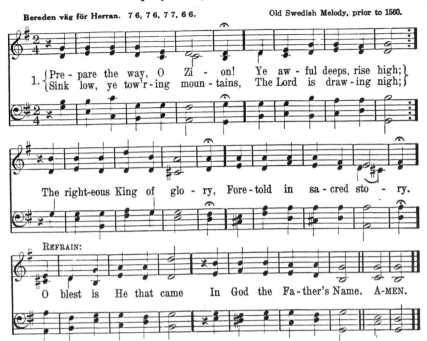

1. {Pre - pare the way, O Zi - on! Ye aw - ful deeps, rise high;}
   {Sink low, ye tow'r - ing moun - tains, The Lord is draw - ing nigh;}

The right-eous King of glo - ry, Fore - told in sa - cred sto - ry.

REFRAIN:

O blest is He that came In God the Fa - ther's Name. A-MEN.

2 O Zion, He approacheth,
　　Thy Lord and King for aye!
　Strew palms where He advanceth,
　　Spread garments in His way.
　God's promise faileth never,
　Hosanna sound forever!

3 Fling wide thy portals, Zion,
　　And hail thy glorious King;
　His tidings of salvation
　　To every people bring,
　Who, waiting yet in sadness,
　Would sing His praise in gladness.

4 He cometh not with warriors,
　　And not with pomp and show,
　Yet smiteth He with terror
　　Sin, death, and every foe.
　The Spirit's sword He wieldeth,
　Not e'en to death He yieldeth.

5 Give heed, thou sinful people,
　　Thy King and Saviour own:
　The kingdom He hath founded
　　Is not an earthly one;
　No power can overthrow it,
　Nor earthly wisdom know it.

6 The throne which He ascendeth
　　Is fixed in heaven above:
　His sanctified dominion
　　Is light alone and love.
　His praise be ever sounding
　For grace and peace abounding.

7 Jerusalem is fallen,
　　And closed its temple-door;
　Its sacrifices ended;
　　Its scepter is no more.
　Christ's kingdom never ceaseth,
　Its glory still increaseth.

Frans Mikael Franzén, 1812.

A classic Swedish Advent hymn, the keynote hymn of the Church Year. The text, which first appeared in the Swedish Psalmbook of 1819, is by Frans Mikael Franzén (1772-1847), renowned Swedish-Finnish pastor and writer. The old Swedish tune goes back to Reformation times, with even earlier roots.

Hymnal (1901) - No.2; *The Hymnal* (1925) - No.1;
Service Book and Hymnal (1958) - No.9; *Lutheran Book of Worship* (1978) - No.26

2

Rejoice, All Ye Believers.

Haf trones lampa färdig. 7 6, 7 6. D.

Swedish Folksong.

1. Re - joice, all   ye   be - liev - ers,   And let   your lights ap - pear!
2. The watch-ers on   the moun - tain   Pro - claim the Bride-groom near;

The eve - ning is   ad - vanc - ing, And dark - er night is   near.
Go meet Him as   He   com - eth, With hal - le - lu - jahs clear.

The Bride-groom is   a - ris - ing,   And soon He draw-eth nigh.
The mar - riage feast is   wait - ing,   The gates wide o - pen stand;

Up, watch, and pray, and wres - tle, — At mid-night comes the cry!
Up, up, ye heirs of   glo - ry,   The Bridegroom is   at hand! A - MEN.

3 Ye saints, who here in patience
  Your cross and sufferings bore,
Shall live and reign forever,
  Where sorrow is no more.
Around the throne of glory
  The Lamb ye shall behold,
In triumph cast before Him
  Your diadems of gold!

4 Our Hope and Expectation,
  O Jesus, now appear;
Arise, Thou Sun so longed for,
  O'er this benighted sphere!
With hearts and hands uplifted,
  We plead, O Lord, to see
The day of earth's redemption,
  That brings us unto Thee!

Laurentius Laurentii, 1700.

An important Advent hymn written by Lorenz Lorenzen (1660-1722), a Danish church musician who Latinized his name to Laurentius Laurenti. It is set to an old Swedish folk melody sometimes called "Vigil."
Hymnal (1901) - No.12; *The Hymnal* (1925) - No.17;
Service Book and Hymnal (1958) - No.14; *Lutheran Book of Worship* (1978) - No.25

O Bride of Christ, Rejoice!

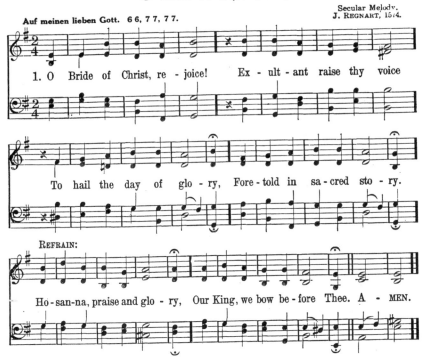

Auf meinen lieben Gott. 6 6, 7 7, 7 7.

Secular Melody.
J. REGNART, 1574.

1. O Bride of Christ, re - joice! Ex - ult - ant raise thy voice

To hail the day of glo - ry, Fore - told in sa - cred sto - ry.

REFRAIN:

Ho - san - na, praise and glo - ry, Our King, we bow be - fore Thee. A - MEN.

2 Let shouts of gladness rise
Triumphant to the skies.
Here comes the King most glorious
To reign o'er all victorious.

3 He wears no kingly crown,
Yet as a king He's known;
Though not arrayed in splendor,
He still makes death surrender.

4 Thy heart now open wide,
Bid Christ with thee abide;
He graciously will hear thee,
And be forever near thee.

5 E'en babes with one accord
With thee shall praise the Lord,
And every gentile nation
Respond with exultation.

Johan Olof Wallin, 1816.

An Advent hymn by Johan Olof Wallin (1779-1839), poet, archbishop and Sweden's greatest hymn writer. The Swedish Psalmbook of 1819 included 342 hymns which he wrote or translated. In the Augustana tradition, the tune for this hymn is by a 16th century German Roman Catholic, Jacob Regnart.

Hymnal (1901) - No.4; *The Hymnal* (1925) - No.18

Now Hail We Our Redeemer.

Förlossningen är vunnen. 7 6, 7 6, 7 7 6.

German Enchiridion, 1524.

1. Now hail we our Re - deem - er, E - ter - nal Son of God,
2. A man, of God be - got - ten, Brought in the age of grace;

Born in the flesh to save us, And cleanse us in His blood.
Lo, all the earth is ra - diant With light, and hope, and peace.

The Morn - ing Star as - cend - eth, Light to the
Our pris - on He de - mol - ished, Death's pow - er

world He lend - eth, Our Guide in grief and gloom.
He a - bol - ished, And o - pened heav - en's gate. A - MEN.

3 O Jesus, grant us mercy,
    And grace on us bestow,
To walk by Thine own guidance,
    Thy saving truth to know.
For Thee our hearts are yearning,
From worldly pleasures turning
    Unto Thy righteousness.

4 Into Thy hand the Father
    Gave all, that we might be
In bonds of faith united,
    And dedicate to Thee,
A people through Thy merit
Entitled to inherit
    Thy realm eternally.

Ambrose, (340-397).
Olavus Petri, 1536.

A translation by the Swedish reformer, Olavus Petri (1493-1552), of an ancient Advent hymn. This text originated with Ambrose of Milan (340-397), the father of Latin hymnody. The tune came to Sweden from Germany.

The Hymnal (1925) - No.21

Hos Gud är idel glädje. 7 6, 7 6. D.   AHNFELTS Sånger.

1. I love to hear the sto - ry Which an - gel voic - es tell,

How once the King of glo - ry Came down on earth to dwell.

I am both weak and sin - ful, But this I sure - ly know,

The Lord came down to save me, Be-cause He loved me so.   A-MEN.

Christmas.

2 I'm glad my blessèd Saviour
　Was once a child like me,
To show how pure and holy
　His little ones should be;
And if I try to follow
　His footsteps here below,
He never will forget me,
　Because He loves me so.

3 To sing His love and mercy
　My sweetest songs I'll raise;
And though I cannot see Him,
　I know He hears my praise;
For He has kindly promised
　That even I may go
To sing among His angels,
　Because He loves me so.

Emily (Huntington) Miller. 1867.

A children's hymn for Christmas set to a tune from an edition of *Andeliga Sånger*, the collection of songs edited by Oskar Ahnfelt (1813-1882), the Swedish pietist who travelled the country singing and playing his ten-string guitar. Emily Huntington Miller (1833-1913), daughter of a Methodist clergyman in Connecticut, wrote the text.   *Hymnal* (1901) - No.30; *The Hymnal* (1925) - No.632

6

25. All Hail to Thee, O Blessed Morn!

Wie schön leuchtet der Morgenstern. 8 8 7, 8 8 7, 8 8 8.

PHILIPP NICOLAI, 1599.

1. All hail to thee, O bless-ed morn! To ti-dings long by prophets borne
2. 'Tis God's own Im-age and, with-al, The Son of Man, that mor-tals all

Hast thou ful-fill-ment giv-en.   O sa-cred and im-mor-tal day,
May find in Him a broth-er.   He comes, with peace and love to bide

When un-to earth, in glo-rious ray, De-scends the grace of heav-en!
On earth, the err-ing race to guide And help as could no oth-er;

Sing-ing, Ring-ing Sounds are blend-ing, Prais-es send-ing
Rath-er Gath-er Clos-er, fond-er, Sheep that wan-der,

Un-to heav-en For the Sav-iour to us giv-en.
Feed and fold them, Than let e-vil pow-ers hold them. A-MEN.

3 He tears, like other men, will shed,
Our sorrows share, and be our aid,
Through His eternal power;
The Lord's good will unto us show,
And mingle in our cup of woe
The drops of mercy's shower;
Dying,
Buying
Through His passion
Our salvation,
And to mortals
Opening the heavenly portals.

4 He comes, for our redemption sent,
And by His glory heaven is rent
To close upon us never;
Our blessèd Shepherd He would be,
Whom we may follow faithfully
And be with Him forever;
Higher,
Nigher
Glory winging,
Praises singing
To the Father
And His Son, our Lord and Brother.

Johan Olof Wallin, 1814.
Based on German Hymn of 1621.

The Swedish Christmas hymn par excellence which always opened the early morning Julotta (*Christmas Day Matins*). The fine text is by Johan Olof Wallin (1779-1839). The tune is the *"Queen of Chorales"* by Philipp Nicolai (1556-1608). *Hymnal* (1901) - No.13; *The Hymnal* (1925) - No.25; *Service Book and Hymnal* (1958) - No.33; *Lutheran Book of Worship* (1978) - No.73

When Christmas Morn Is Dawning.

När juldagsmorgon glimmar. 7 6, 7 6.

German Folksong.

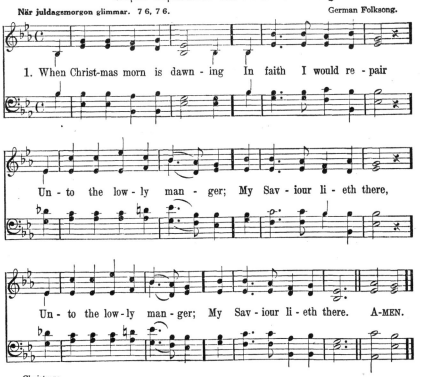

1. When Christ-mas morn is dawn - ing In faith I would re - pair

Un - to the low - ly man - ger; My Sav - iour li - eth there,

Un - to the low - ly man - ger; My Sav - iour li - eth there. A - MEN.

Christmas.

2 How kind, O loving Saviour,
To come from heaven above!
From sin and evil save us,
And keep us in Thy love.

3 We need Thee, blessèd Jesus,
Our dearest friend Thou art;
Forbid that we by sinning
Should grieve Thy loving heart.

Hemlandssånger.

A classic Christmas hymn for children first published in Sweden in 1851. All Swedish-American hymnals included this hymn whose text is probably German in origin. The tune is a German folk melody which Johannes Brahms used in his Academic Festival Overture. *Hymnal* (1901) - No.27;
The Hymnal (1925) - No.635;
Service Book and Hymnal (1958) - *No.35; Lutheran Book of Worship* (1978) - No.59

Thou Didst Leave Thy Throne.

Margaret. Irregular.

TIMOTHY RICHARD MATTHEWS, 1876.

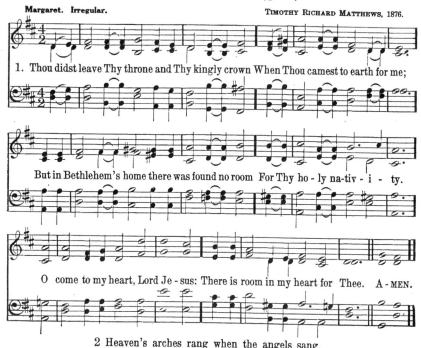

1. Thou didst leave Thy throne and Thy kingly crown When Thou camest to earth for me;

But in Bethlehem's home there was found no room For Thy ho - ly na-tiv - i - ty.

O come to my heart, Lord Je - sus: There is room in my heart for Thee. A - MEN.

2 Heaven's arches rang when the angels sang,
　　Proclaiming Thy royal degree;
　　But in lowly birth didst Thou come to earth,
　　　And in great humility.
　　O come to my heart, Lord Jesus:
　　There is room in my heart for Thee.

3 The foxes found rest, and the bird had its nest
　　In the shade of the forest tree;
　　But Thy couch was the sod, O Thou Son of God,
　　　In the mountains of Galilee.
　　O come to my heart, Lord Jesus:
　　There is room in my heart for Thee.

4 Thou camest, O Lord, with the living Word
　　That should set Thy children free;
　　But with mocking scorn, and with crown of thorn,
　　　They bore Thee to Calvary.
　　O come to my heart, Lord Jesus:
　　There is room in my heart for Thee.

5 When the heavens shall ring, and the angels sing
　　At Thy coming to victory,
　　Let Thy voice call me home, saying, "Yet there is room,
　　　There is room at my side for thee."
　　And my heart shall rejoice, Lord Jesus,
　　When Thou comest to call for me.

Emily Elizabeth Steele Elliott, 1864.

A Victorian children's hymn by an English writer, Emily E. S. Elliot (1836-1897). Much-loved in Augustana circles and still popular in England, it emphasizes our Lord's emptying himself of divine power
when he came to earth.
The Hymnal (1925) - No. 47;
Service Book and Hymnal (1958) - No. 433

Du lifvets bröd. 8 7, 8 7, 8 8 7.   PETER SOHREN, 1668.

1. Thou go-est to Je-ru-sa-lem, O Son of God, to suf-fer, And for a world of sin-ful men Thy spot-less life to of-fer; Thou bear-est an-guish, pain, and loss, The mock-ers' scorn, the scourge, the cross, To win for us sal-va-tion. A-MEN.

2 Before Thee lies Gethsemane,
   The scene of bitter anguish;
Thine eyes behold the Calvary
   Where Thou in pain must languish;
The bleeding wounds, the bitter gall,
The crown of thorns, the judgment hall,
   Thy burdened soul's affliction.

3 Thou art the Way, the Truth, the Life;
   We pray Thee, Master, lead us
Away from earth's vain, restless strife;
   With heavenly manna feed us.
Thou who hast died to save the lost,
Help us, dear Lord, to weigh the cost,
   And follow Thee, our Saviour.

Anna Hoppe, 1921.

A hymn for Quinquagesima, the Sunday before Ash Wednesday, but suitable for Lent. The text is by Anna Hoppe (1889-1941), a gifted Lutheran poet from Wisconsin who wrote 23 hymns published in the Augustana hymnal of 1925. The tune, by Peter Sohren (1632-1692), came to Sweden from Germany.

The Hymnal (1925) - No.83

Thy Cross, O Jesus, Thou Didst Bear.

So gehst du nun, mein Jesu, hin. 8 7, 8 7, 4 4 7. Iambic.

CASPER FRIEDRICH NACHTENHÖFER, 1651.

1. Thy cross, O Je - sus, Thou didst bear, And yield Thy-self an of - f'ring
2. Thy cross, Re-deem-er, Thou didst bear, When all had Thee for-sak - en;

To save a sin - ful world which e'er With scorn be-holds Thy suf - f'ring.
My sins and guilt Thou bor - est there, Thy love hath me o'er-tak - en!

O wondrous love From heav'n above, To bleed for Thine ac-cus - ers!
Thou callest me To come to Thee And be Thy child for-ev - er. A - MEN.

3 Thy cross, O Saviour, Thou didst bear:
  Thy boundless might and glory,
  Forever praised by angels fair,
  And told in sacred story,
  Thou didst resign,
  O love divine
  That conquereth in dying!

4 Thy cross to victory Thou didst bear;
  O grant that I, dear Saviour,
  May glory in the cross and share
  Thy heavenly joy and favor!
  Then shall my soul
  Have reached its goal,
  Safe in Thy loving bosom.

Erik Gustaf Geijer, 1812.

A hymn for Holy Week by Erik Gustav Geijer (1783-1847), poet and professor at Uppsala University in Sweden. The tune is an 18th century German chorale by Kaspar-Friedrich Nachtenhöfer (1624-1685).
Hymnal (1901) - No.72; *The Hymnal* (1925) - No.105

Sweet the Moments, Rich in Blessing.

11

Gnadauer Choralbuch, 1784.
Batty (Ringe recht wenn Gottes Gnade). 8 7, 8 7. Har. by WILLIAM HENRY MONK, (1823-1889).

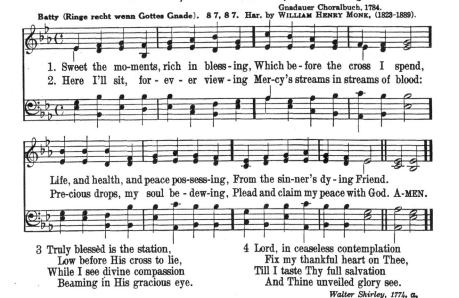

1. Sweet the mo-ments, rich in bless-ing, Which be-fore the cross I spend,
2. Here I'll sit, for - ev - er view-ing Mer-cy's streams in streams of blood:

Life, and health, and peace pos-sess-ing, From the sin-ner's dy-ing Friend.
Pre-cious drops, my soul be - dew-ing, Plead and claim my peace with God. A-MEN.

3 Truly blessèd is the station,
  Low before His cross to lie,
  While I see divine compassion
  Beaming in His gracious eye.

4 Lord, in ceaseless contemplation
  Fix my thankful heart on Thee,
  Till I taste Thy full salvation
  And Thine unveiled glory see.

Walter Shirley, 1774, a.

With text by an English writer, this hymn is set to a Moravian tune. Walter Shirley (1725-1786), an Anglican clergyman, adapted it from a text by James Allen (1734-1804). The melody is used in the communion liturgy of the Moravian Church and sung to many hymn texts.
  Hymnal (1901) - No.69; *The Hymnal* (1925) - No.109; *Service Book and Hymnal* (1958) - No.63

My Crucified Saviour, Despised and Contemned.

Min blodige konung. 11 11, 11 11.

ANDREAS CARL RUTSTRÖM, (1721–1772).

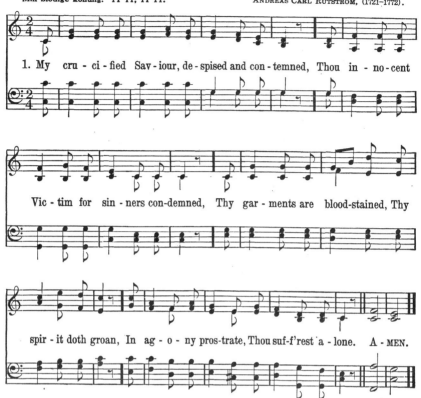

1. My cru - ci - fied Sav - iour, de - spised and con - temned, Thou in - no - cent

Vic - tim for sin - ners con - demned, Thy gar - ments are blood-stained, Thy

spir - it doth groan, In ag - o - ny pros-trate, Thou suf-f'rest a - lone. A - MEN.

2 Thou weepest and moanest in conflict and prayer,
And writhest in agony, pain, and despair;
In thirty years' anguish our path Thou hast trod,
And diest at last to redeem us to God.

3 Our Saviour thus finished God's plan with our race,
And laid the foundation for pardon and grace.
And then rose triumphant, the conquering Lord,
Appeased the Creator and mankind restored.

4 Restored to the bliss that was lost in the fall,
Yea, greater, for Jesus prepared for us all
Eternal salvation and mansions above;
Come, poor, burdened sinners, rejoice in His love.

5 Yea, come, trembling sinner, come just as thou art,
Thy cares and thy sorrows to Jesus impart;
In Him seek salvation from death and the grave,
For Jesus is willing and mighty to save.

Andreas Carl Rutström, (1721–1772)

One of the finest pietistic hymns of the 18th century with text by Fredrika Falck (1719-1749), a Swedish pastor's wife, with a tune probably composed by Andreas Carl Rutström (1721-1772). Often called simply "Lenten Hymn," it shows the strong influence of the Moravians on Swedish pietism.

Hymnal (1901) - No.77; *The Hymnal* (1925) - No. 114

Gorton. S. M.

Arranged from BEETHOVEN, 1807.

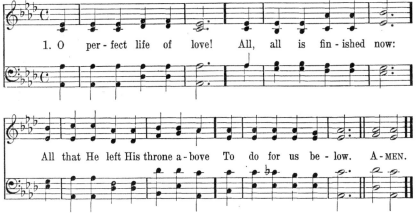

1. O per - fect life of love! All, all is fin - ished now:

All that He left His throne a - bove To do for us be - low. A - MEN.

2 No work is left undone
  Of all the Father willed;
  His toil, His sorrows, one by one,
  The Scripture have fulfilled.

3 No pain that we can share
  But He has felt its smart;
  All forms of human grief and care
  Have pierced that tender heart.

4 In perfect love He dies;
  For me He dies, for me;
  O all-atoning Sacrifice,
  I cling by faith to Thee.

5 Work, then, O Lord, in me,
  As Thou for me hast wrought;
  And let my love the answer be
  To grace Thy love has brought.

Henry Williams Baker, 1875.

A Victorian hymn set to a tune arranged from a theme by Ludwig van Beethoven (1770-1827). The words are by Henry Williams Baker (1821-1877), a Church of England clergyman who edited the first edition of *Hymns Ancient and Modern.*

The Hymnal (1925) - No.118; *Service Book and Hymnal* (1958) - No.89

The Saviour Is Risen.

Hvad ljus öfver griften! 6 5, 6 5, 6 5, 6 5, 6 5, 6 5, 6 4.

NIELS JESPERSON'S Gradual, 1573.

1. { The Sav-iour is ris-en, Light bursts from the tomb; The liv-ing ful-
   { A-dored by the an-gels, The Vic-tor comes forth To claim for His

fill-ment Of Scrip-ture is come. } The seal has been bro-ken, The
king-dom The ran-somed on earth. }

stone rolled a-way, And fled are the watch-ers In fear and dis-

may; Hell trem-bles be-fore Him. Hal-le-lu-jah. A-MEN.

2 Light grappled with darkness,
    Death wrestled with life;
Now light comes triumphant
    From out the dread strife.
While death lieth vanquished,
    Hope kindles again
The torch of the faithful
    To shine among men.
Ye sorrowing women
    Who hither have sped,
Why seek ye the living
    To-day 'mongst the dead?
For Jesus is risen.
    Hallelujah.

3 Now God in His heaven
    And man are at one,
The grave is a pathway,
    Through Christ, to the throne.
Ye friends that are bending
    In grief at the cross,
Now lift your heads gladly,
    Ye suffered no loss.
O flock, scattered widely,
    Return to the fold:
Thy Shepherd still liveth,
    And now as of old
He leadeth thee Godward.
    Hallelujah.

4 'Mid storms and upheavals
   His Church stands secure.
The truth of His gospel
   Shall ever endure.
Lo! unto all peoples
   His message shall speed,
Proclaiming 'mid turmoil
   The Lord's mighty deed,
Proclaiming the Saviour
   Who died for all men,
And, having arisen,
   Now liveth again,
Firstfruits of the sleeping.
   Hallelujah.

5 Then weep not, ye faithful,
   Yield not to despair:
The night soon is over,
   The day shall appear.
Though earth shall embrace you
   When death lays you low,
The seed of His sowing
   To harvests will grow;
And soon shall the Sower
   Return to His field
With angels to gather
   Its heavenly yield,
From evil tares severed.
   Hallelujah.

Frans Mikael Franzén, 1811.

This classic Swedish Easter hymn by Franz Mikael Franzén (1772-1847), expresses clearly the ancient atonement doctrine of Christ as Victor. The tune is from Niels Jesperson's Gradual (1573), an early hymn collection from Denmark. This hymn was known as "He liveth forever!" in the Augustana hymnal of 1901.
Hymnal (1901) - No.83; *The Hymnal* (1925) - No.123

Blest Easter Day, What Joy Is Thine.

Lob sei dem allmächtigen Gott. L. M.

JOHANN CRÜGER, 1640.

1. Blest Eas - ter day, what joy is thine! We praise, dear
2. The tree where Thou wast of - fered up Now bears the

Lord, Thy Name di - vine, For Thou hast tri - umphed o'er the
fruit of life and hope: Thy pre - cious blood for us is

tomb; No more we need to dread its gloom.
shed, Now we may feed on heav'n - ly bread. A - MEN.

3 We thank Thee, Jesus, that Thy hand
Has freed us from sin's galling band;
No more its thralldom we need fear;
The year of liberty is here.

4 O Jesus Christ, God's Son elect,
Our Paschal Lamb without defect,
To us Thou givest strength indeed,
In all our conflicts, all our need.

5 O grant that, as Thou didst arise,
We, too, with joy may heavenward rise,
First from our sin, to love Thy way,
Then from the grave on that great Day.

6 All praise to Thee who from death's might,
From carnal lust and sin's dark plight
Redeemest me, that even I
May reach eternal life on high.

Olavus Petri, 1536.

An early Easter hymn by the Swedish Reformer, Olavus Petri (1493-1552), who studied with Luther in Wittenberg. It is set to a chorale by Johann Crüger (1598-1662), a famous German composer who strongly influenced Swedish hymnody. *Hymnal* (1901) - No.80; *The Hymnal* (1925) - No.125

Upp, min tunga, 4 4 7, 4 4 7, 4 4 7.

Koralbok, 1697.

1. Praise the Sav - iour Now and ev - er! Praise Him all be -
2. Man's work fail - eth, Christ's a - vail - eth, He is all our

neath the skies! Pros - trate ly - ing, Suf - f'ring, dy - ing
Right - eous - ness. He our Sav - iour Hath for - ev - er

On the cross, a Sac - ri - fice; Vic - t'ry gain - ing,
Set us free from dire dis - tress. Through His mer - it

Life ob - tain - ing, Now in glo - ry He doth rise.
We in - her - it Light, and peace, and hap - pi - ness. A - MEN.

3 Sin's bonds severed,
    We're delivered,
Christ hath bruised the serpent's head;
    Death no longer
    Is the stronger,
Hell itself is captive led.
    Christ hath risen
    From death's prison,
O'er the tomb He light hath shed.

4 For His favor,
    Praise forever
Unto God the Father sing;
    Praise the Saviour,
    Praise Him ever,
Son of God, our Lord and King;
    Praise the Spirit,
    Through Christ's merit,
He doth us salvation bring.

Venantius Honorius Clementianus Fortunatus, (530?–609).

A Swedish adaptation of a famous Latin hymn by Venantius Fortunatus (530-609). Johan Olof Wallin revised and shortened it, moving it from the Passion section to the Easter section of the 1816 *Svenksa Psalmboken.* The anonymous melody, sometimes called "Riddarholm", first appeared in Sweden in 1697.

Hymnal (1901)-No.90; *The Hymnal* (1925) - No.135

Service Book and Hymnal (1958) - No.104; *Lutheran Book of Worship* (1978) - No.155

18 Hail, Thou Once Despiséd Jesus!

Lammets folk och Sions fränder. 8 7, 8 7. D.   ANDREAS CARL RUTSTRÖM, (1721–1772).

1. Hail, Thou once de-spis-éd Je-sus! Hail, Thou Ga-li-le-an King!
   Thou didst suf-fer to re-lease us; Thou didst free sal-va-tion bring.

Hail, Thou ag-o-niz-ing Sav-iour, Bear-er of our sin and shame!

By Thy mer-its we find fa-vor; Life is giv-en through Thy Name. A-men.

2 Paschal Lamb, by God appointed,
  All our sins on Thee were laid;
  By almighty love anointed,
  Thou hast full atonement made.
All Thy people are forgiven,
  Through the virtue of Thy blood:
  Opened is the gate of heaven;
  Peace is made 'twixt man and God.

2 Jesus, hail, enthroned in glory,
  There forever to abide!
All the heavenly hosts adore Thee,
  Seated at Thy Father's side:

There for sinners Thou art pleading,
  There Thou dost our place prepare,
  Ever for us interceding,
  Till in glory we appear.

4 Worship, honor, power, and blessing,
  Thou art worthy to receive;
  Loudest praises, without ceasing,
  Meet it is for us to give.
Help, ye bright angelic spirits,
  Bring your sweetest, noblest lays,
  Help to sing our Saviour's merits,
  Help to chant Immanuel's praise.

JOHN BAKEWELL, (1721–1819), 1757. Altered.

A classic hymn for Ascension Day by John Bakewell (1721-1819), an English Methodist. The source of its popular Swedish revival tune is unknown, although it is attributed to Andreas Carl Rütstrom (1721-1772).
Hymnal (1901) - No.98; *The Hymnal* (1925) – No. 149;
Service Book and Hymnal (1958) – No.435

Machs mit mir, Gott, nach deiner Güt. 8 7, 8 7, 8 8.   JOHANN HERMANN SCHEIN, 1627.

1. To realms of glo-ry I be-hold My ris-en
2. Far from my home—how long, dear Lord, Be-fore my

Lord re-turn-ing; While I, a stran-ger in the earth,
ex-ile end-eth? But far be-yond the realms of sense

For heav'n am ev-er yearn-ing. Far from my heav'n-ly
My fer-vent prayer as-cend-eth: My prayer, un-ut-tered,

Fa-ther's home, 'Mid toil and sor-row here I roam.
but a groan, Shall rend the skies and reach Thy throne. A-MEN.

3 Then visions of the goodly land
     By faith my soul obtaineth;
   There I shall dwell for evermore
     Where Christ in glory reigneth,
   In mansions of that blest abode,
   The city of the living God.

4 In that blest city is no night,
     Nor any pain or weeping;
   There is my treasure, there my heart,
     Safe in my Saviour's keeping;
   In heaven, my blessèd Lord, with Thee,
   May all my conversation be.

5 In glory He shall come again
     To earth as He ascended;
   So let me wait and watch and pray,
     Until my day is ended.
   That day, O Lord, is hid from me,
   But daily do I wait for Thee.

6 And blessèd shall that servant be,
     O Lord, at Thy returning,
   Whose heart is waiting, Lord, for Thee,
     Whose lamp is trimmed and burning;
   Him wilt Thou take to dwell with Thee
   In joy and peace eternally.

Johan Olof Wallin, 1816.

This hymn focuses on the Ascension and Second Coming of Christ. The text is by Johan Olof Wallin (1779-1839), the archbishop who was Sweden's greatest hymn writer. The famous German composer, Johann Hermann Schein (1586-1630), wrote this chorale tune which Bach included in the St John Passion.
Hymnal (1901) - No.94; The *Hymnal* (1925) - No.146

Holy Ghost, Dispel Our Sadness.

Jesus är min vän den bäste. 8 7, 8 7. D.

GUSTAF DÜBEN, 1674.

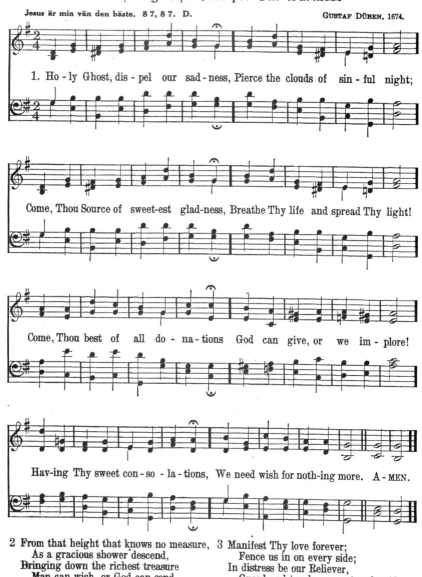

1. Ho - ly Ghost, dis - pel our sad - ness, Pierce the clouds of sin - ful night;

Come, Thou Source of sweet-est glad-ness, Breathe Thy life and spread Thy light!

Come, Thou best of all do - na - tions God can give, or we im - plore!

Hav-ing Thy sweet con - so - la - tions, We need wish for noth-ing more. A - MEN.

2 From that height that knows no measure,
  As a gracious shower descend,
Bringing down the richest treasure
  Man can wish, or God can send.
Author of the new creation!
  Come with unction and with power;
Make our hearts Thy habitation;
  On our souls Thy graces shower.

3 Manifest Thy love forever;
  Fence us in on every side;
In distress be our Reliever,
  Guard and teach, support and guide.
Hear, O hear our supplication,
  Loving Spirit, God of peace!
Rest upon this congregation,
  With the fullness of Thy grace.

Paul Gerhardt, 1653.

A Pentecost hymn by the great German Lutheran hymn-writer, Paul Gerhardt (1607-1676). The tune is by Gustaf Düben (1628-1690), who was royal court music-master and organist at the German church in Stockholm. He became a leading personality in 17th century Swedish musical life.

Hymnal (1901) - No.103; *The Hymnal* (1925) - No.155

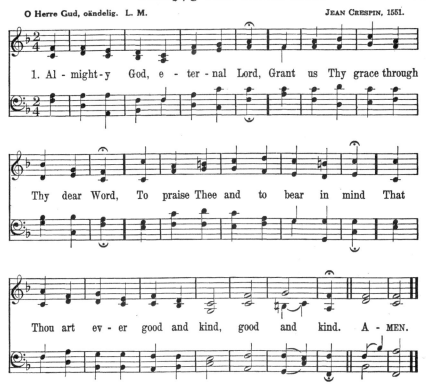

O Herre Gud, oändelig. L. M.   JEAN CRESPIN, 1551.

1. Al - might-y God, e - ter - nal Lord, Grant us Thy grace through

Thy dear Word, To praise Thee and to bear in mind That

Thou art ev - er good and kind, good and kind. A - MEN.

2 Lord Jesus Christ, incarnate Word,
   Thy Name be evermore adored,
   For all Thine anguish, death, and pain,
   Whereby salvation we obtain.

3 O Holy Spirit, grant us grace,
   And guide us in Thy righteous ways,
   That we may with the heavenly host
   Praise Father, Son, and Holy Ghost.

Johan Olof Wallin, 1816.

A hymn for Trinity by Johan Olof Wallin (1779-1839), the archbishop and poet who was Sweden's greatest hymn writer, called "David's Harp in the Northland" by national poet Esais Tegnér. The tune is from the Reformation period.   *Hymnal* (1901) - No.113; *The Hymnal* (1925) - No.167

Glory to the Father Give.

Sabbatsdag, hur skön du är. 7 7, 7 7.

JOEL BLOMQVIST.

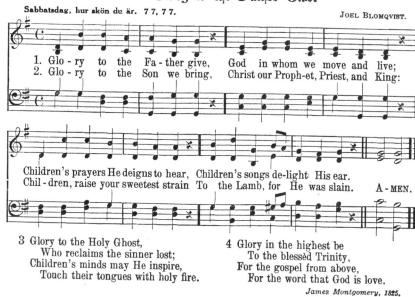

1. Glo - ry to the Fa - ther give, God in whom we move and live;
2. Glo - ry to the Son we bring, Christ our Proph-et, Priest, and King:

Children's prayers He deigns to hear, Children's songs de-light His ear.
Chil - dren, raise your sweetest strain To the Lamb, for He was slain. A - MEN.

3 Glory to the Holy Ghost,
　Who reclaims the sinner lost;
　Children's minds may He inspire,
　Touch their tongues with holy fire.

4 Glory in the highest be
　To the blessèd Trinity,
　For the gospel from above,
　For the word that God is love.

James Montgomery, 1825.

A children's hymn celebrating the Trinity by James Montgomery (1771-1854), the great Moravian hymn writer from Britain. Joel Blomqvist (1840-1930), a hymn writer and composer from the Swedish free church tradition, wrote the tune. *Hymnal* (1901) - No.115; *The Hymnal* (1925) - No.640

Thy Sacred Word, O Lord, of Old.

O Gud! ditt rike ingen ser. 8 7, 8 7. D.

BURKHARD WALDIS, 1553.

1. Thy sa-cred Word, O Lord, of old Was veiled a-bout and dark-ened,
And in its stead were leg-ends told, To which the peo-ple hark-ened;
Thy Word, for which the faith-ful yearned, The world-lings kept in hid-ing,
And in-to hu-man fa-bles turned Thy truth, the all-a-bid-ing. A-MEN.

2 Now thanks and praise be to our Lord,
  Who boundless grace bestoweth,
And daily through the sacred Word
  His precious gifts forthshoweth.
His Word is come to light again,
  A trusty lamp to guide us;
No strange and divers teachings then
  Bewilder and divide us.

Olavus Petri, (1497-1552).

A militant Reformation hymn by Olavus Petri (1493-1552), the Swede who brought the reformation faith to Sweden from Wittenberg, where he studied with Luther. Burkhard Waldis (c1490-1557), a German monk who became a Lutheran pastor and composer during the Reformation, wrote this chorale tune.

The Hymnal (1925) - No.215

Mein Seel, o Herr, muss loben dich. L. M.

BARTHOLOMÄUS GESIUS, 1601.

1. The death of Je-sus Christ, our Lord, We cel-e-
2. He blot-ted out with His own blood The judg-ment

brate with one ac-cord; It is our com-fort in dis-
that a-gainst us stood; He full a-tone-ment for us

tress, Our heart's sweet joy and hap-pi-ness.
made, And all our debt He ful-ly paid. A-MEN.

3 That this is so and ever true
He gives an earnest, ever new,
In this His holy Supper, here
We taste His love, so sweet, so near.

4 For His true body, as He said,
And His true blood, for sinners shed,
In this communion we receive:
His sacred Word we do believe.

5 A precious food is this indeed,
It never faileth; such we need,
A heavenly manna for our soul,
Until we safely reach our goal.

6 Then blest is every worthy guest
Who in this promise findeth rest,
For Jesus will in love abide
With those who do in Him confide.

7 O sinner, come with true intent
To turn to God and to repent,
To live for Christ, to die to sin,
And thus a holy life begin.

8 Who does unworthy here appear,
Does not believe, nor is sincere,
Salvation here can never find.
May we this warning bear in mind.

9 O Jesus Christ, our Brother dear,
Unto Thy cross we now draw near;
Thy sacred wounds indeed make whole
A wounded and afflicted soul.

10 Help us sincerely to believe
That we Thy mercy do receive,
And in Thy grace do find our rest,
Amen. He who believes is blest.

Haquin Spegel, 1686.

A classic communion hymn by Haquin Spegel (1654-1714), who worked with Jesper Swedberg on a controversial Swedish hymnbook used extensively in the New Sweden colony in America. It is set to a chorale by a German theologian and church musician, Bartholomäus Gesius (c1555-1613).

Hymnal (1901) - No.222; *The Hymnal* (1925) - No.234

O Jesu! än de dina. 76, 76, 876.

HANS THOMISSÖNS PSALMEBOG, 1569.

1. Thine own, O lov-ing Sav-iour, Thou bid-dest come to Thee,
2. To us on earth still dwell-ing Thou dost de-scend to give,

Thy pas-sion's fruits, Thy fa-vor, Thy grace, Thou giv-est free
In love all love ex-cel-ling, Thy-self that we may live,

To them who by Thy grace and love Are mem-bers
And say-est, ev-er kind and good: "Take, eat, this

of Thy king-dom, Now here, and then a-bove.
is My bod-y, Take, drink, this is My blood." A-MEN.

3 We hear Thine invitation;
  We hear, O Lord, Thy call,
The word of consolation,
  It is for us, for all;
It draws us to Thy loving heart,
  It brings to us Thy blessing,
  It does Thy peace impart.

4 Thy heart is in all anguish
  A refuge to the poor,
Thy heart for us did languish,
  And bitter death endure.
Thy heart, yet filled with peace and rest,
  With comfort and salvation,
Draws near to every breast.

5 Thou still in loving favor
  To us, Thine own, art near,
To lead us as our Saviour
  Unto a Father dear,
A Father willing to forgive
  The children Thou didst ransom,
And who through Thee shall live.

6 We are Thine own forever;
  Until our latest breath
Will we be true, and never
  In joy, in grief, in death,
Depart from Thee, for Thou always
  Art present with Thy people,
As Thine own promise says.

Frans Mikael Franzén, 1814.

Perhaps the most often used communion hymn in the Augustana hymnal, with text by Franz Mikael Franzén (1772-1847), a Swedish-Finnish pastor and poet. The translation is by Olof Olsson (1841-1900), a president of Augustana College and Theological Seminary. The tune is believed to be Danish in origin, but its roots go back to Germany.   *Hymnal* (1901) - No.223; *The Hymnal* (1925) - No.235; *Service Book and Hymnal* (1958) - No.264; *Lutheran Book of Worship* (1978) - No.496

According to Thy Gracious Word.

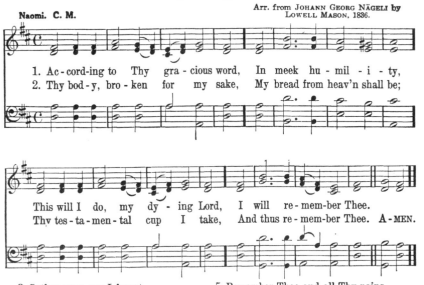

Naomi. C. M.

Arr. from JOHANN GEORG NÄGELI by
LOWELL MASON, 1836.

1. Ac-cord-ing to Thy gra-cious word, In meek hu-mil-i-ty,
2. Thy bod-y, bro-ken for my sake, My bread from heav'n shall be;

This will I do, my dy-ing Lord, I will re-mem-ber Thee.
Thy tes-ta-men-tal cup I take, And thus re-mem-ber Thee. A-MEN.

3 Gethsemane can I forget,
   Or there Thy conflict see,
Thine agony and bloody sweat,
   And not remember Thee?

4 When to the cross I turn mine eyes,
   And rest on Calvary,
O Lamb of God, my Sacrifice!
   I must remember Thee.

5 Remember Thee and all Thy pains,
   And all Thy love to me;
Yea, while a breath, a pulse remains,
   Will I remember Thee.

6 And when these failing lips grow dumb,
   And mind and memory flee,
When Thou shalt in Thy kingdom come.
   O Lord, remember me!

James Montgomery, 1825.

A Moravian communion hymn which was a favorite in Augustana circles. The text is by James Montgomery (1771-1854) a renowned hymn writer born in Scotland. The tune is by Johann Georg Nägeli (1773-1836), a Swiss music educator. It was arranged by Lowell Mason (1792-1872), an American hymn writer and music educator from Massachusetts.

Hymnal (1901) - No.230; *The Hymnal* (1925) - No.239;
Service Book and Hymnal (1958) - No.266

Come, O Jesus, and Prepare Me.

Jesus är min vän den bäste. 8 7, 8 7. D.

GUSTAF DÜBEN, 1674.

1. Come, O Je - sus, and pre - pare me Now to be Thy wor - thy guest.

Like Thy well be - lov'd dis - ci - ple, Let me lean up - on Thy breast

At Thy ta - ble, where Thou giv - est Of Thy bod - y and Thy blood,

Seal - ing in this blest com-mun - ion My bap - tis-mal vow to God. A-MEN.

First Communion of Catechumens.

2 Take my heart and make it holy
  By Thy Spirit and Thy grace;
Back into Thy footsteps guide me,
  If I stray in evil ways.
Thou who lovèdst me from childhood,
  Be my Refuge in my youth;
In a world where error lures me,
  Lead me in Thy paths of truth.

3 Let me heed Thy voice entreating,
  "Come, my child, abide with Me;
Wouldst thou spurn the loving-kindness
  Of the Friend who died for thee?"
Grant that, at Thy sacred altar,
  Through Thy sacrament of grace,
With the faithful I be numbered,
  And Thy saving love embrace.

Frans Mikael Franzén, 1814.

A hymn often used for the first communion of catechumens. The text is by Swedish-Finnish poet and bishop, Frans Mikael Franzén (1772-1847). This classic tune is by Gustaf Düben (1628-1690), a leading musician in 17th century Sweden. *The Hymnal* (1925) - No.245

A Voice, A Heavenly Voice I Hear!

ST. JAMES' STOCKHOLM. 8 8 6, 8 8.   OLOF AHLSTRÖM, 1756–1835

With joyful dignity

1. A voice, a heaven - ly voice I hear! A - rise, O soul, come
2. I come, dear Je - sus, at thy word, A guest un - wor - thy

and draw near To hal - low and re - vere The day the Lord thy
to thy board, My Sav - iour and my Lord. O clothe me with thy

God doth make, And of the bread of life par - take.
right - eous - ness, My soul with thy sal - va - tion bless! A - men.

3 O Lord, who my Redeemer art,
Come thou and purify my heart.
From thee I'll ne'er depart,
But wheresoe'er thou leadest me
In constant faith I'll follow thee. Amen.

Johan Olof Wallin, 1779–1839
Tr. 1, 2, Composite
Tr. St. 3, Ernst W. Olson, 1870–

A communion hymn of invitation by Johan Olof Wallin (1779-1830), the great Swedish archbishop and hymn writer. The tune by Olof Ahlström (1756-1835) , is also Swedish.   *The Hymnal* (1925) - No. 238;
Service Book and Hymnal (1958) - No. 270

Take the Name of Jesus with You.

Take the Name. 8 7, 8 7. With Refrain.

WILLIAM HOWARD DOANE, 1871.

1. Take the Name of Je - sus with you, Child of sor - row and of woe;
2. Take the Name of Je - sus ev - er, As a shield from ev - 'ry snare;

It will joy and com - fort give you, Take it, then, wher-e'er you go.
If temp - ta - tions round you gath - er, Breathe that ho - ly Name in prayer.

REFRAIN:

Pre-cious Name, O how sweet, Hope of earth and joy of heav'n!

Pre-cious Name, O how sweet, Hope of earth and joy of heav'n! A-MEN.

Copyright, 1899, by W. H. Doane, in renewal. Used by permission.

3 O the precious Name of Jesus!
How it thrills our souls with joy,
When His loving arms receive us,
And His songs our tongues employ.

4 At the Name of Jesus bowing,
Falling prostrate at His feet,
King of kings in heaven we'll crown Him,
When our journey is complete.

Lydia Baxter, 1871.

An early American Gospel song, based on Philippians 2:9-11 with words by Lydia Baxter (1809-1874), who wrote many songs for Sunday schools and evangelistic services. The tune is by William Howard Doane (1832-1915), a Baptist Sunday school superintendent from Ohio.

Hymnal (1901) - No.37; *The Hymnal* (1925) - No.260

Zion Stands with Hills Surrounded.

Jesus, låt din rädda dufva. 8 7, 8 7, 4 4 7.

Swedish Folk Melody.

1. Zi - on stands with hills sur-round-ed; Zi - on kept by pow'r di - vine:

All her foes shall be con-found-ed, Though the world in arms com-bine.

Hap-py Zi - on, Hap-py Zi - on, What a fa-vored lot is thine! A - MEN.

2 Every human tie may perish;
  Friend to friend unfaithful prove;
Mothers cease their own to cherish;
  Heaven and earth at last remove:
    But no changes
Can attend Jehovah's love.

3 In the furnace God may prove thee,
  Thence to bring thee forth more bright,
But can never cease to love thee;
  Thou art precious in His sight:
    God is with thee,
God, thine everlasting Light.

Thomas Kelly, 1806.

With text by the great Irish hymn writer, Thomas Kelly (1769-1855), this hymn about the church is set to a Swedish folk tune of unknown origin. This tune is usually called "Tillflykt" (Refuge) and appeared in *Sionstoner* (Melodies of Zion), a Swedish revivalist hymnbook published in 1889.

Hymnal (1901) - No.185; *The Hymnal* (1925) - No.262

Agatha. 8 8 7, 8 8 7.   CARL JOHANNES SÖDERGREN, 1924.

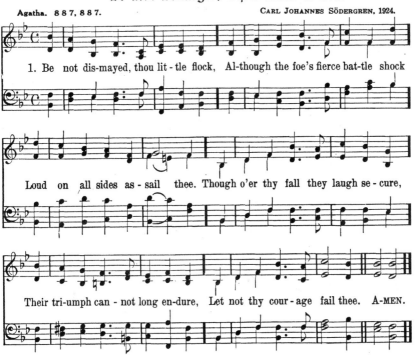

1. Be not dis-mayed, thou lit - tle flock, Al-though the foe's fierce bat-tle shock

Loud on all sides as - sail thee. Though o'er thy fall they laugh se - cure,

Their tri-umph can - not long en-dure, Let not thy cour - age fail thee. A-MEN.

2 Thy cause is God's—go at His call,
And to His hand commit thine all;
Fear thou no ill impending;
His Gideon shall arise for thee,
God's Word and people manfully
In God's own time defending.

3 Our hope is sure in Jesus' might;
Against themselves the godless fight,
Themselves, not us, distressing;
Shame and contempt their lot shall be;
God is with us, with Him are we;
To us belongs His blessing.
Johann Michael Altenburg, 1632.

King Gustavus II Adolphus of Sweden sang this hymn the day he died in the battle of Lützen in 1632. Most likely the author was German Lutheran pastor, Johann Michael Altenburg (1584-1640). It is set to a tune by Carl Johannes Södergren (1870-1949), professor at Augustana Seminary and the Lutheran Bible Institute.
Hymnal (1901) - No.190; *The Hymnal* (1925) - No. 263

With God and His Mercy, His Spirit, and Word.

Ack, saliga stunder. 11 11 11, 6 6 11.   OSKAR AHNFELT, (1813-1882).

1. With God and His mer - cy, His Spir - it, and Word, And lov - ing com-mun-ion at al - tar and board, We meet with as - sur-ance the dawn of each day: The Shep-herd is with us, The Shep-herd is with us, To lead and pro - tect us, and teach us the way. A - MEN.

2 In perilous times, amid tempests and night,
A band presses on through the gloom
toward light;
Though humble, and meek, and disowned
by the world,
They follow the Saviour,
And march on to glory, with banners
unfurled.

3 While groveling worldlings with dross
are content,
And ever on sin and transgression are
bent,
I follow, victorious hosts, at your word,
And march on to glory,
We march on to glory, our captain the Lord.

4 The sign of the cross I triumphantly bear,
Though none of my kindred that emblem
may wear;
I joyfully follow the champions of right,
Who march on to glory,
Who march on to glory, with weapons of
might.

5 O Shepherd, abide with us, care for us still,
And feed us and lead us and teach us
Thy will;
And when in Thy heavenly fold we shall
be,
Our thanks and our praises,
Our thanks and our praises we'll render
to Thee.

Carl Olof Rosenius, (1816-1868).

A highly popular Swedish hymn by Carl Olof Rosenius (1816-1868) with a tune by Oskar Ahnfelt (1813-1882). This hymn was a special favorite of the early Swedish immigrants in the United States and has been called "the revivalist Marseillaise of all middle-Sweden." It emphasizes the contrast between Christians and the world.

Hymnal (1901) - No.196; *The Hymnal* (1925) - No.272; *Lutheran Book of Worship* (1978) - No. 371

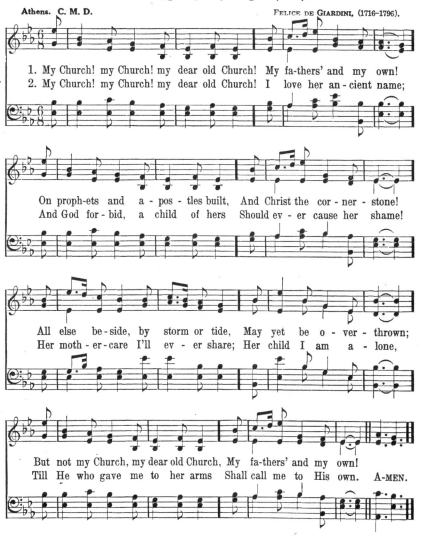

Athens. C. M. D.

FELICE DE GIARDINI, (1716-1796).

1. My Church! my Church! my dear old Church! My fa-thers' and my own!
2. My Church! my Church! my dear old Church! I love her an-cient name;

On proph-ets and a - pos - tles built, And Christ the cor - ner - stone!
And God for - bid, a child of hers Should ev - er cause her shame!

All else be-side, by storm or tide, May yet be o - ver - thrown;
Her moth - er-care I'll ev - er share; Her child I am a - lone,

But not my Church, my dear old Church, My fa-thers' and my own!
Till He who gave me to her arms Shall call me to His own.   A-MEN.

3 My Church! my Church! I love my Church,
 For she doth lead me on
To Zion's palace beautiful,
 Where Christ my Lord hath gone.
From all below she bids me go
 To Him, the Life, the Way,
The Truth to guide my erring feet
 From darkness into day.

4 Then here, my Church! my dear old Church!
 Thy child would add a vow,
To that whose token once was signed
 Upon his infant brow:—
Assault who may, kiss and betray,
 Dishonor and disown,
My Church shall yet be dear to me,
 My fathers' and my own!

Anonymous.

This hymn, though not of Swedish origin in text or tune, was much-loved in Augustana for its expression of the Swedish and Augustana Lutheran idea of the church. The author is unknown. The tune is from a work by an Italian baroque composer, Felice Giardini (1716-1796).

Hymnal (1901) - No.189; *The Hymnal* (1925) - No. 276

Come, Saviour Dear, with Us Abide.

Kom, huldaste förbarmare. 8 7, 8 7, 8 8 7.   FREDRIK GABRIEL HEDBERG, (1811-1893).

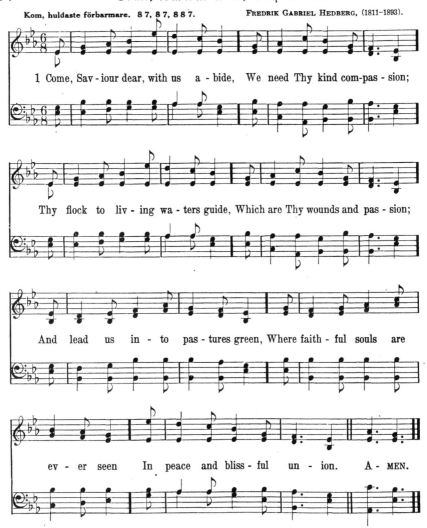

1 Come, Sav - iour dear, with us a - bide, We need Thy kind com-pas - sion;
Thy flock to liv - ing wa - ters guide, Which are Thy wounds and pas - sion;
And lead us in - to pas - tures green, Where faith - ful souls are
ev - er seen In peace and bliss - ful un - ion. A - MEN.

2. O Sea of love, pour out Thy flood
   O'er all in blessèd showers;
The fiery darts quench with Thy blood,
   And crush hell's evil powers.
Thou, of the world the Mercy-Seat,
Let of Thy love the gentle heat
   Set all our hearts aglowing.

Andreas Carl Rutström, (1721-1772).

This 18th century pietistic hymn is by Andreas Carl Rutström (1721-1772) who was strongly influenced by the Moravians (Herrnhuters). It focuses on the blood of Christ as the agent of atonement. Frederik Gabriel Hedberg (1811-1893) composed this melody a century later.

Hymnal (1901) - No. 149; *The Hymnal* (1925) - No.298.

Werde munter, mein Gemüthe. 8 7, 8 7, 7 7, 8 8.   JOHANN SCHOP, 1642.

1. Guard-ian of pure hearts, and Hear-er, Lord, of ev-'ry faith-ful prayer,
2. With the right-eous oft it far-eth Here as if his deeds were ill;

In Thy courts one day is dear-er Than a thou-sand days else-where.
Blight fair vir-tue's flow'rs im-pair-eth, Weeds of vice do flour-ish still;

Worn with earth's un-rest, how sweet In Thy tem-ple fair to meet!
Joy and for-tune haste a-way, Friends with friends—how short their stay!

There to sing a-way each sor-row That from life and toil we bor-row!
Rach-el still her children mourneth, And her soul from comfort turn-eth. A-MEN.

3 But when here devoutly soareth
   High the temple-anthem sweet,
   Grief grows calm, no plaint outpoureth,
      Hearts with holy rapture beat:
   Free from earthly clouds, the soul
   Presses toward a higher goal,
   Takes from hope the comfort given,
   Speaks e'en now the tongue of heaven.

4 O my soul, on wings ascending,
   Thou on Salem's mount shalt rest;
   There where cherub-harps are blending
      With the singing of the blest:
   Let thy note of praise and prayer
   To thy God precede thee there,
   While e'en yet a careworn mortal,
   Still without thy Father's portal.

5 Christians, while on earth abiding,
   Let us ever praise and pray,
   Firmly in our God confiding,
      As our fathers in their day;
   Be the children's voices raised
   To the God their fathers praised.
   Let His bounty, failing never,
   Be on us and all forever.

6 Bless us, Father, and protect us,
   Be our souls' sure hiding-place,
   Let Thy wisdom still direct us,
      Light our darkness with Thy grace!
   Let Thy countenance on us shine,
   Fill us all with peace divine.
   Praise the Father, Son, and Spirit,
   Praise Him all that life inherit.

Johan Olof Wallin, 1816.

The final two verses of this hymn by Johan Olof Wallin (1779-1839) are particularly treasured. The sixth
verse is a paraphrase of the Aaronic benediction by Jesper Svedberg (1653-1735), the father of Emmanuel
Swedenborg, the mystic and philosopher. It is set to a famous chorale used often by J. S. Bach.

Hymnal (1901) - No. 158; The Hymnal (1925) - No.313;
Service Book and Hymnal (1958) - No.462; *Lutheran Book of Worship* (1978) - No.440

Wachet auf. 8 9 8, 8 9 8, 6 6 4, 8 8.   PHILIPP NICOLAI, 1599.

1. Ho - ly Maj - es - ty, be - fore Thee We bow to wor-ship and a - dore Thee;
2. God of light, ex - alt - ed, ho - ly! Thy ten - der care pro-tects the low - ly,

With grate-ful hearts to Thee we sing. Earth and heav-en tell the sto - ry
Nor leaves Thy chil-dren to their fate. Gra-cious art Thou, God our Fa - ther,

Of Thine e - ter-nal might and glo - ry, And all Thy works their in-cense bring.
Thy cho - sen peo-ple Thou dost gath - er With - in Thine arms com-pas-sion-ate.

Lo, hosts of Cher - u - bim And count-less Ser - a - phim Sing, Ho - san - na,
Thou gav-est us Thy Son, Thro' whom Thy grace is won, And Thy Spir - it

Ho - ly is God, al-might-y God, All-mer - ci - ful and all-wise God!
Dwelleth with-in to cleanse from sin Whom Thine own Son hath died to win. A - MEN.

Choirs of faithful voices name Thee,
And all Thy chosen seed proclaim Thee,
Most holy, holy, holy Lord.
Hear Thy ransomed children praying
That we may do Thy will, ne'er straying
Away from Thee, nor from Thy Word.
Vouchsafe to us Thy love,
Thy wisdom from above;
Grant us, Father,
That in its light we walk aright
In holiness as in Thy sight.

4 Bless and keep, O Lord, Thy creatures,
Reveal to us Thy gracious features,
O turn to us Thy face with peace.
Here our songs we humbly tender,
Till glorified our tongues shall render
To Thee our praise without surcease,
Where hosts of Cherubim
And countless Seraphim
Sing, Hosanna,
Holy is God, almighty God,
All-merciful and all-wise God!

Samuel Johan   Hedborn, 1812.

The King of Chorales", by Philipp Nicolai (1556-1608) is the tune for this hymn of praise by Samuel J. edborn (1783-1849), a Swedish pastor and hymn-writer, who suffered from bouts of depression. Ten of s hymns were included in the 1819 *Svenska Psalmboken.*   *The Hymnal* (1925) - No.315;
Service Book and Hymnal (1958) - No.189; *Lutheran Book of Worship* (1978) - No.247

Jehovah, Thee We Glorify.

Vi lofve dig, o store Gud. 8 8, 4 6, 10.

Rostockerhandboken, 1529.

1. Je - ho - vah, Thee we glo -, ri - fy, Rul - er up - on Thy
2. Thou car - est gen - tly for Thy flock; Thy Church, firm-found - ed

throne on high! O let Thy Word Thro' all the earth be heard.
on the Rock, No pow'rs dis - may Un - til Thy dread - ful day.

Ho - ly, ho - ly, ho - ly art Thou, O Lord.
Ho - ly, ho - ly, ho - ly art Thou, O Lord. A - MEN.

3 All nations, in her fold comprised,
  Shall bow their knees unto the Christ,
    All tongues shall raise
    Their orisons and praise:
  Holy, holy, holy art Thou, O Lord.

4 Around Thy throne the countless throng
  At last in triumph swell the song,
    When Cherubim
    Shall answer Seraphim:
  Holy, holy, holy art Thou, O Lord.

Johan Olof Wallin, 1816.

This Swedish version of the *Te Deum laudamus*, arranged by Johan Olof Wallin (1779-1836), picks up the theme of the *Trisagion* ("Holy, holy, holy") with which the Swedish Mass of 1819 begins. The tune, also called "Ter Sanctus", was first used in *Een ny Handbog*, one of the earliest Danish-Norwegian Lutheran hymnals, published in 1529.   *The Hymnal* (1925) - No.316

Service Book and Hymnal - No.174; *Lutheran Book of Worship* (1978) - No.432

Mine Eyes unto the Mountains.

Old 130th Psalm. 7 6, 7 6. D. **Genevan Psalter, 1556.**

1. Mine eyes un - to the moun - tains I lift, whence help goes forth;

My help comes from Je - ho - vah, Mak - er of heav'n and earth.

Thy foot shall nev - er fal - ter; Thy ev - 'ry step He keeps;

The Lord who keep-eth Is - rael, He slum-bers not, nor sleeps. A - MEN.

2 The shade of the Almighty
　Shields thee upon the right.
The sunlight shall not smite thee,
　Nor shall the moon by night.
Thy coming in He blesseth,
　And from the temple door
Thy going out He guideth
　Now and forevermore.

Ernst William Olson, 1922.

This paraphrase of Psalm 121 is by Ernst William Olson (1870-1958), a writer and poet who worked at Augustana Book Concern for more than 30 years. The tune is from the Reformed tradition and was found in the French Psalter in Strasbourg in 1539.

The Hymnal (1925) - No.323;
Service Book and Hymnal (1958) - No.398

Our Mighty God Works Mighty Wonders

40

1. Our might-y God works might-y won-ders— what joy to
2. God's might-y Word goes forth to con-quer, its pow'r de-
3. Be-hold a host of saints are near-ing the gates of
4. Dear Lord, as throngs your king-dom en-ter, may not my

see them all a-round! All i-dols fall be-fore his thun-ders,
stroys the forts of doubt; the war-riors bold yield up their ar-mor
heav'n with might-y tread; with ban-ners wav-ing, sing-ing, cheer-ing,
heart your love de-cline; teach me my faith on you to cen-ter,

their al-tars crum-bling to the ground. God breaks the
to him who will not cast them out. They cleans-ing
they hail in joy their roy-al Head; and man-y
draw me to you by grace di-vine. Take now my

fet-ters, frees the slaves, his fall-en chil-dren still he saves.
find in Je-sus' blood and laud and mag-ni-fy our God.
more shall own God's reign, his won-drous love the vic-t'ry gain.
hand and hold it fast, un-til I reach your heav'n at last.

WORDS: Nils Frykman, 1842-1911, tr. A. L. Skoog, 1856-1934, Andrew T. Frykman, 1875-1943, alt.
MUSIC: Swedish melody

9.8.9.8.8.8.
CELEBRATION

Although not in any English-language Augustana hymnals, the text for this hymn is in the *Söndagsskolbok* (1903) and the *Lutherförbundets Sängbok* (1913), both published by the Augustana Book Concern. Nils Frykman (1842-1911), a hymn writer of the Mission Covenant Church, wrote the words which are set to a Swedish folk tune. *Hemlandssånger* (1892) – No.288; *Hymnal* (1901) – No.294 (tune); *Söndagsskolbok* (1903) – No.119; *Lutherförbundets Sångbok* (1913) – No.140

O Lord, Give Heed unto Our Plea.

**41**

Af himlens här den högstes makt. 8 7, 8 7, 8 8 7.

Swedish, 1697.

1. O Lord, give heed un-to our plea, O Spir-it, grant Thy grac-es,

That we who put our trust in Thee May right-ly sing Thy

prais-es. Thy Word, O Christ, un-to us give, That grace and

pow'r we may re-ceive To fol-low Thee, our Mas-ter. A-MEN.

2 Touch Thou the shepherd's lips, O Lord,
That in this blessèd hour
He may proclaim Thy sacred Word
With unction and with power.
What Thou wouldst have Thy servant say,
Put Thou into his heart, we pray,
With grace and strength to say it.

3 Let heart and ear be opened wide
Unto Thy Word and pleading;
Our minds, O Holy Spirit, guide
By Thine own light and leading.
The law of Christ we would fulfill,
And walk according to His will,
His Word our rule of living.

Jesper Swedberg.

An entrance hymn by Bishop Jesper Svedberg (1643-1735), an early Swedish hymnwriter. His hymnal of 1694 was rejected by the Church of Sweden on theological grounds. Many copies were shipped to the Swedish colonists who lived along the Delaware River in America, for whom Svedberg had episcopal oversight. This tune was also found in Svedberg's hymnal.   *The Hymnal* (1925) - No.348

Tell Me the Old, Old Story.

Evangel. 7 6, 7 6. D. With Refrain.

WILLIAM HOWARD DOANE, 1869.

1. Tell me the old, old story Of un-seen things a - bove;
2. Tell me the sto - ry slow - ly, That I may take it in—

Of Je - sus and His glo - ry, Of Je - sus and His love.
That won-der - ful re - demp - tion, God's rem-e - dy for sin.

Tell me the sto - ry sim - ply, As to a lit - tle child;
Tell me the sto - ry oft - en, For I for - get so soon;

For I am weak and wea - ry, And help - less and de - filed.
The ear - ly dew of morn - ing Has passed a - way at noon.

REFRAIN:

Tell me the old, old sto - ry, Tell me the old, old sto - ry,

Tell me the old, old sto - ry, Of Je - sus and His love. A-MEN.

Used by permission of W. H. Doane.

3 Tell me the story softly,
　　With earnest tones and grave;
　Remember, I'm the sinner
　　Whom Jesus came to save.
　Tell me that story always,
　　If you would really be,
　In any time of trouble,
　　A comforter to me.

4 Tell me the same old story,
　　When you have cause to fear
　That this world's empty glory
　　Is costing me too dear;
　And when the light of heaven
　　Is dawning on my soul,
　Tell me the old, old story:
　　"Christ Jesus makes thee whole."

Katherine Hankey, 1866.

A popular Gospel hymn by Anabella Katherine Hankey (1834-1911) who was part of an evangelical group in the Church of England called the Clapham Sect. William Howard Doane (1832-1915), a prolific hymn writer who was a Baptist from Ohio, composed the tune.

Hymnal (1901) - No.217; *The Hymnal* (1925) - No. 351

44. In the Temple Where Our Fathers.

Werde munter, mein Gemüthe. 8 7, 8 7, 7 7, 8 8.　　　　　JOHANN SCHOP, 1642.

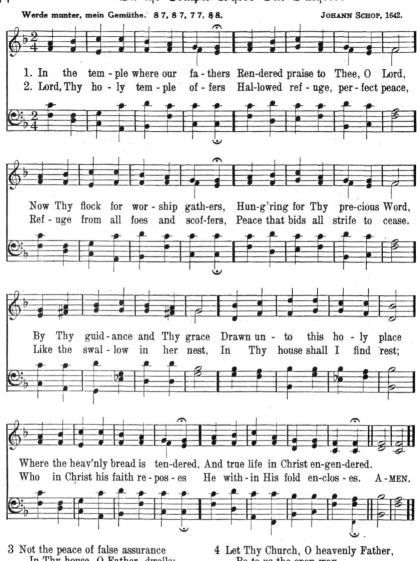

1. In the tem - ple where our fa - thers Ren-dered praise to Thee, O Lord,
2. Lord, Thy ho - ly tem - ple of - fers Hal-lowed ref - uge, per - fect peace,

Now Thy flock for wor - ship gath-ers, Hun-g'ring for Thy pre-cious Word,
Ref - uge from all foes and scof-fers, Peace that bids all strife to cease.

By Thy guid-ance and Thy grace Drawn un - to this ho - ly place
Like the swal - low in her nest, In Thy house shall I find rest;

Where the heav'nly bread is ten-dered, And true life in Christ en-gen-dered.
Who in Christ his faith re - pos - es He with - in His fold en-clos - es. A - MEN.

3 Not the peace of false assurance
　In Thy house, O Father, dwells;
There the strength for our endurance
　From Thy sacred altar wells.
　　To Thy presence we draw nigh,
　　Grant us power from on high;
With Thy sword and helmet arm us,
That no worldly foes alarm us.

4 Let Thy Church, O heavenly Father,
　Be to us the open way
To that temple where we gather
　Round Thy throne some blessèd day.
　　Gentle Shepherd, as of old,
　　Feed us, tend us, in Thy fold,
And at last Thy flock deliver,
In Thy heaven to dwell forever.

Erik Natanael Söderberg, (b. 1869).

This hymn of prayer and praise for the beginning of worship is by Erik Natanael Söderberg (1869-1937), writer and publisher. It expresses the reverence Swedes felt for their church buildings. The famous chorale tune is by Johann Schop (c.1590-1667), a famous musician and composer from northern Germany.

The Hymnal (1925) - No.349

God be with you. 9 8, 8 9. With Refrain. WILLIAM GOULD TOMER, 1882.

1. God be with you till we meet a-gain, By His coun-sels guide, up-hold you,

With His sheep se-cure-ly fold you, God be with you till we meet a-gain.

REFRAIN:

Till we meet, ... till we meet, . . Till we
Till we meet, till we meet, till we meet,

meet at Je-sus' feet; Till we meet, . . . till we
Till we meet; Till we meet, till we

meet, God be with you till we meet a-gain. A-MEN.
meet, till we meet,

Copyright by J. E. Rankin.

2 God be with you till we meet again,
'Neath His wings protecting hide you,
Daily manna still divide you,
God be with you till we meet again.

Jeremiah Eames Rankin, 1882.

A gospel song by Jeremiah Eames Rankin (1828-1904), an American Congregational minister who was once president of Howard University in Washington, D.C. The Moody and Sankey hymn collection helped make it popular in many countries. Hardly a literary masterpiece, it has strong emotional appeal. William Gould Tomer composed the melody in 1882, the year when the words were written.

The Hymnal (1925) - No.364

Ajar the Temple Gates Are Swinging.

Wer weiss, wie nahe mir mein Ende. 9 8, 9 8, 8 8.   BRONNER'S Choral-Buch, 1715.

1. A - jar the tem - ple gates are swing - ing, Lo! still the grace of God is free. Per - haps when next the bells are ring - ing The grave shall o - pen un - to thee, And thou art laid be - neath the sod No more to see this house of God. A - MEN.

2 But if to-day the Lord thou seekest,
　His blessèd gospel to embrace,
He who gives strength unto the weakest
　Shall fill thy heart with truth and grace.
In life He will thy footsteps guide,
In death He still is at thy side.

3 O come to-day, and do not reckon
　Upon the day that is not thine.
The Lord in mercy still doth beckon:
　Accept to-day His grace divine.
Then shall thy prayers and praises rise
A sacred incense to the skies.

Frans Mikael Franzén, 1814.

A hymn by Frans Mikael Franzén (1772-1847), bishop and colleague of Wallin, often used as an opening hymn. It is a classic expression of orthodox pietism's call to salvation and evokes the church bells of both a Swedish church and many rural and small town Augustana churches. It is set to a well-known German chorale.

The Hymnal (1925) - No.402

Schmücke dich, o liebe Seele. L. M. D.

JOHANN CRÜGER, 1649.

Bless - ed, bless - ed he who know - eth That His faith on Thee is
found - ed, Whom the Fa - ther's love be - stow - eth Of e - ter - nal
grace un - bound - ed, Je - sus Christ, to ev - 'ry na - tion
A Re - deem - er free - ly giv - en, In whose Name is
our sal - va - tion, And none else in earth or heav - en. A - MEN.

Johan Olof Wallin, 1816.

Almost a creedal statement of Christocentric faith by Johan Olof Wallin (1779-1839), this hymn was often sung before the sermon. The familiar chorale tune is by the German church musician, Johann Crüger 1598-1662), who wrote hymns and edited hymn books.

The Hymnal (1925) - No.417;
Service Book and Hymnal (1958) - No.381

48

I Look Not Back.

O sälla land. 11 10, 11 10.   OSKAR AHNFELT, (1813–1882).

1. I look not back; God knows the fruit-less ef-forts, The wast-ed hours, the sin-ning, the re-grets. I leave them all with Him who blots the rec-ord, And gra-cious-ly for-gives, and then for-gets. A-MEN.

2 I look not forward; God sees all the future,
  The road that, short or long, will lead me home,
And He will face with me its every trial,
  And bear for me the burdens that may come.

3 I look not round me; then would fears assail me,
  So wild the tumult of earth's restless seas,
So dark the world, so filled with woe and evil,
  So vain the hope of comfort and of ease.

4 I look not inward; that would make me wretched;
  For I have naught on which to stay my trust.
Nothing I see save failures and shortcomings,
  And weak endeavors, crumbling into dust.

5 But I look up—into the face of Jesus,
  For there my heart can rest, my fears are stilled;
And there is joy, and love, and light for darkness,
  And perfect peace, and every hope fulfilled.

Unknown.

A pietistic expression of objective faith in Christ by an unknown Swedish author. The tune is by Oskar Ahnfelt (1813-1882), whose hymns gained immense popularity during the 19th century revival. The famous singer, Jenny Lind, provided funds for the first edition of his *Andeliga Sånger* (Spiritual Songs). *The Hymnal* (1925) - No.431

Oss kristna bör tro och besinna. 9 8, 9 8, 9 9 8.   Swedish Melody, known 1540.

1. We Christians should ev - er con - sid - er What Christ hath so gra-cious-ly
2. All na - ture a   ser-mon may preach thee; The birds sing thy mur-murs a-

taught; For He who hath made us His chil - dren Would have us re-
way; The birds, which, nor sow-ing nor reap - ing, God fails not to

tain in our thought How lit - tle things earth-ly do mer - it, Lest we, who should
feed day by day; And He who those creatures doth cher-ish, He nev - er will

heav - en in - her - it, The heav-en - ly prize leave un-sought.
leave thee to per - ish; For art thou not bet - ter than they? A - MEN.

3 The lilies, nor toiling nor spinning,
   Their clothing how gorgeous and fair!
 What tints in their tiny robes woven,
   What wondrous devices are there!
 All Solomon's stores could not render
 One festival robe of such splendor
   As modest field lilies do wear.

4 If God o'er the grass and the flowers
   Such delicate beauty hath spread,—
 The flowers which to-day are so fragrant,
   To-morrow are faded and dead,—
 O why, then, should earthly cares fret thee?
 Thy Father will never forget thee,
   Nor fail to provide thee with bread.

Haquin Spegel, 1686.

A hymn by Haquin Spegel (1645-1714), Swedish bishop and hymn writer. Based on Jesus' words in Matthew 6, this hymn is set to a 16th century Swedish melody. This is a classic statement of creation spirituality in a distinctively Lutheran mode. *Hymnal* (1901) - No.297; *The Hymnal* (1925) - No.445

Jesus, Keep Me Near the Cross.

Near the Cross. 7 6, 7 6. Trochaic. With Refrain.   WILLIAM HOWARD DOANE, (1831–1915).

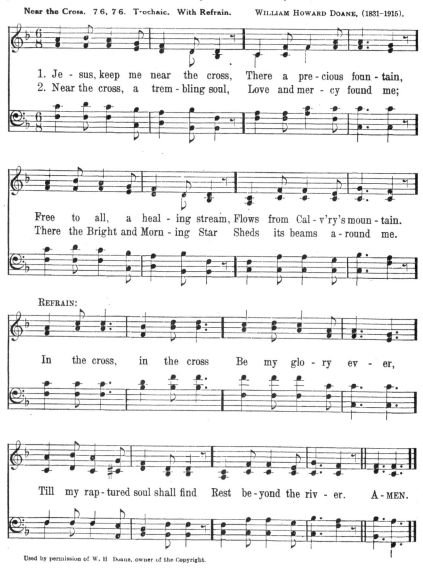

1. Je - sus, keep me near the cross, There a pre-cious foun-tain,
2. Near the cross, a trem-bling soul, Love and mer-cy found me;

Free to all, a heal-ing stream, Flows from Cal - v'ry's moun-tain.
There the Bright and Morn-ing Star Sheds its beams a-round me.

REFRAIN:

In the cross, in the cross Be my glo-ry ev-er,

Till my rap-tured soul shall find Rest be-yond the riv-er. A-MEN.

Used by permission of W. H. Doane, owner of the Copyright.

3 Near the cross! O Lamb of God,
  Bring its scenes before me;
  Help me walk from day to day
  With its shadows o'er me.

4 Near the cross I'll watch and wait,
  Hoping, trusting ever,
  Till I reach the golden strand
  Just beyond the river.

Frances Jane (Crosby) Van Alstyne, 1869.

A Gospel hymn by the blind poet, Fanny Jane Crosby (1832-1915), who may be America's best-known hymn writer. It is set to a melody by the popular hymn composer, William H. Doane (1823-1915).
Hymnal (1901) - No.281; *The Hymnal* (1925) - No.46

I Need Thee Every Hour.

I need Thee. 6 4, 6 4. With Refrain.

ROBERT LOWRY, 1872.

1. I need Thee ev - 'ry hour, Most gra - cious Lord,

No ten - der voice like Thine Can peace af - ford.

REFRAIN:

I need Thee, O I need Thee, Ev - 'ry hour I need Thee:

O bless me now, my Sav - iour, I come to Thee. A - MEN.

2 I need Thee every hour,
   Stay Thou near by;
   Temptations lose their power
   When Thou art nigh.

3 I need Thee every hour,
   In joy or pain;
   Come quickly and abide,
   Or life is vain.

4 I need Thee every hour,
   Teach me Thy will;
   And Thy rich promises
   In me fulfill.

5 I need Thee every hour,
   Most Holy One,
   O make me Thine indeed,
   Thou blessèd Son.

Annie Sherwood Hawks, 1872.

A hymn tune Robert Lowry (1826-1899), a leader in the 19th century American gospel song movement, wrote while serving as a Baptist minister in Brooklyn, NY. A member of his congregation, Annie Sherwood Hawks (1835-1918), wrote the words. The refrain is by Lowry. *Hemlandssånger (1892)-No.313; Hemlandssånger (1892)-No.313; Hymnal (1901) - No.285; The Hymnal (1925) - No.462; Service Book and Hymnal (1958) - No.479*

52 All the Way My Saviour Leads Me.

All the way. 8 7, 8 7. D. ROBERT LOWRY, (1826-1899).

1. All the way my Sav-iour leads me; What have I to ask be - side?

Can I doubt His ten-der mer - cy, Who thro' life has been my Guide?

Heav'n-ly peace, di - vin-est com - fort, Here by faith in Him to dwell!

For I know, what-e'er be - fall me, Je - sus do - eth all things well;

For I know what-e'er be - fall me, Je - sus do - eth all things well. A - MEN.

2 All the way my Saviour leads me,
  Cheers each winding path I tread,
Gives me grace for every trial,
  Feeds me with the living bread.
Though my weary steps may falter,
  And my soul athirst may be,
Gushing from the Rock before me,
  Lo! a spring of joy I see.

3 All the way my Saviour leads me;
  O the fullness of His love!
Perfect rest to me is promised
  In my Father's house above.
When my spirit, clothed immortal,
  Wings its flight to realms of day,
This my song through endless ages:
  Jesus led me all the way.

Frances Jane (Crosby) Van Alstyne, (1820-1915).

Another much-loved gospel hymn by Fanny Jane Crosby (1823-1915), the blind poet who may be America's best-known hymn writer. It is set to a tune by Robert Lowry (1826-1899), a Baptist minister who wrote much gospel music in the 19th century. *The Hymnal* (1925) - No.464

Jesus! du dig själf uppväckte. 8 7, 8 7, 8 7 7.   Swedish, 1695.

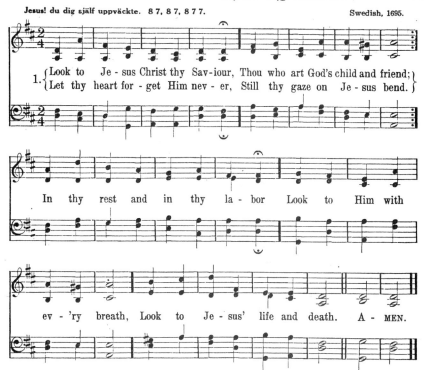

1. { Look to Je-sus Christ thy Sav-iour, Thou who art God's child and friend; }
   { Let thy heart for-get Him nev-er, Still thy gaze on Je-sus bend. }

In thy rest and in thy la-bor Look to Him with

ev-'ry breath, Look to Je-sus' life and death. A-MEN.

2 Look to Jesus, till reviving
   Faith and love thy bosom swell;
Strength for all things good deriving
   From Him who did all things well;
Work as He did, in thy season,
Works which shall not fade away,
Work while it is called To-day.

3 Look to Jesus, praying, waking,
   When thy feet on roses tread;
Follow, worldly pomp forsaking,
   With thy cross where He hath led.
Look to Jesus in temptation;
Baffled shall the tempter flee,
And God's angels come to thee.

4 Look to Jesus, when dark lowering
   Perils thy horizon dim;
Unlike His disciples cowering,
   Calm 'mid tempests look on Him.
Trust in Him who still rebuketh
Wind and billow, fire and flood;
Forward! then, and trust in God.

5 Look to Jesus when distressèd,
   See what He, the Sinless, bore;
Is thy heart with conflict pressèd?
   Is thy soul still harassed sore?
See His bloody sweat, His conflict,
Watch His agony increase,
Hear His prayer, and taste His peace!

6 Art thou by sore want surrounded?
   Do thy pains press forth thy sighs?
Art thou wronged and deeply wounded?
   Does a scornful world despise?
Friends forsake thee or deny thee?
See what Jesus must endure,
He who as the light was pure!

7 Look to Jesus still to shield thee,
   When this dwelling thou must leave;
In that last need He will yield thee
   Peace the world can never give.
Look to Him, thy head low bending;
He, who finished all for thee,
Takes thee then with Him to be.

Frans Mikael Franzén, 1816.

A hymn of faith in Christ through all of life's experiences by Frans Mikael Franzén (1772-1847), the Swedish-Finnish bishop who wrote many classic hymns. The tune is a chorale *Then Swenska Psalmboken,* 1695.

The Hymnal (1925) - No.467

Jesus Is My Friend Most Precious.

Jesus är min van den bäste. 8 7, 8 7. D.

GUSTAF DÜBEN, 1674.

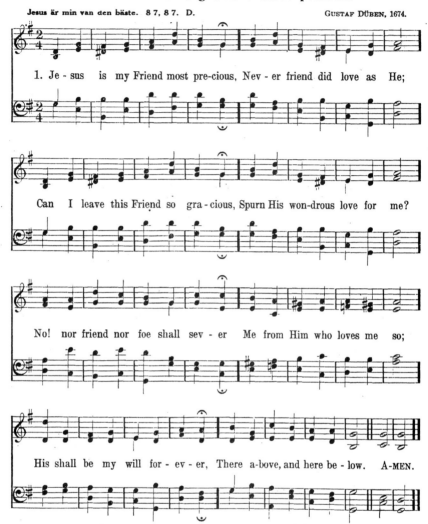

1. Je - sus is my Friend most pre-cious, Nev - er friend did love as He;

Can I leave this Friend so gra-cious, Spurn His won-drous love for me?

No! nor friend nor foe shall sev - er Me from Him who loves me so;

His shall be my will for - ev - er, There a-bove, and here be - low. A-MEN.

2 Bitter death for me He suffered;
    From all guilt He set me free;
  To His Father He hath offered
    Everlasting prayers for me.
  Who is he that would condemn me?
    Christ hath saved me by His grace;
  Who can from my Saviour draw me?
    I am safe in His embrace.

3 Now I am convincèd that never
    Life or death can sever me
  From my blessèd Lord and Saviour;
    Present things, nor things to be,
  Height nor depth, nor fear nor favor,
    Naught that heaven or earth affords
  Makes the sacred promise waver:
    "Ye are Christ's, and He's the Lord's."

Jacob Arrhenius, 1691.

Jakob Arrhenius (1642-1725), professor of history at Uppsala University, was also a sensitive Christian poet. He wrote this hymn which emphasizes the love of Jesus for us. The tune is by Gustaf Düben (1628-1690), a leading musicologist and composer in 17th century Sweden. *Hymnal* (1901) - No.302; *Söndagsskolbok* (1903) - No.108; *The Hymnal* (1925) - No.470

Freu dich sehr, o meine Seele. 8 7, 8 7, 7 7, 8 8.   French Psalter, 1555.

1. Je - sus, in my walk and liv - ing, Let me ev - er fol - low Thine;
2. Let Thy pre - cepts be my guid-ance, Shin-ing on my gloom - y way;

Bear - er of the cross, O teach me Pa - tient - ly to take up mine.
Hold - ing to Thy blest ex - am - ple, Who can err or go a - stray?

If by fel - low men de - spised, Make me like to Thee, O Christ,
Thou who ful - ly didst ful - fill For our sake Thy Fa - ther's will,

O'er their sins and er - rors griev-ing, And all in - jur - ies for - giv-ing.
Help me so to live that nev - er Aught from Thee my soul shall sev - er. A-MEN.

3 In my joys and in my sorrows,
　　Teach Thou me that perfect faith
Which, in trustful prayer persistent,
　　Wavers not in life or death.
My will unto Thine I yield;
With Thy Word and Spirit filled,
Let my life to Thee be given:
Service here, and praise in heaven.

4 For my task, O Lord, equip me
　　From Thy store of rich supply,
That the world and all its evils
　　I may in Thy strength defy.
Willing, yet in body weak,
I Thy safe protection seek;
Perfect strength in weakness give me,
In Thy saving arms receive me.

Johan Hjertén, 1816.

A devotional hymn of faith by Johan Hjertén (1781-1835), an obscure country pastor from Hellstad, Sweden. Six of his hymns were included in the 1819 *Psalmbok.* The melody is a Reformed psalm tune from the 16th century.

The Hymnal (1925) - No.475

Hela världen fröjdes Herran! 8 7, 8 7, 7 7.   Swedish, 1689.

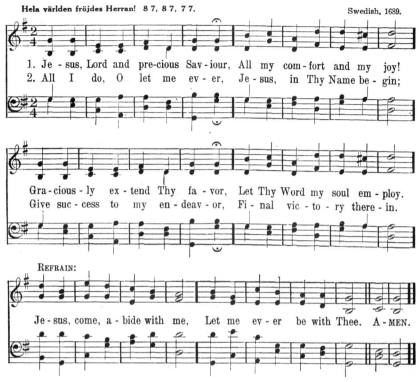

1. Je - sus, Lord and pre-cious Sav - iour, All my com - fort and my joy!
2. All I do, O let me ev - er, Je - sus, in Thy Name be - gin;

Gra - cious - ly ex - tend Thy fa - vor, Let Thy Word my soul em - ploy.
Give suc - cess to my en - deav - or, Fi - nal vic - to - ry there - in.

REFRAIN:

Je - sus, come, a - bide with me, Let me ev - er be with Thee. A - MEN.

3 Let my words and thoughts, O Saviour,
  To Thy praise and glory tend;
  Help me, Lord, that I may gather
  Treasures that shall never end.

4 When my days on earth are over,
  Let me enter into rest.
  Bear me home, O blessèd Saviour,
  When to Thee it seemeth best.

Johan Olof Wallin, 1819.

A translation by Jakob Arrhenius (1642-1725) of a German hymn which has remained popular through the years. The Swedish immigrants to the United States brought it with them and included it in many songbooks. A handwritten copy of this 17th century Swedish melody is in the library at Västerås.

Hymnal (1901) - No.301; *The Hymnal* (1925) - No.482;
Service Book and Hymnal (1958) - No.485

Children of the Heavenly Father.

Tryggare kan ingen vara. L. M.

Swedish Folksong.

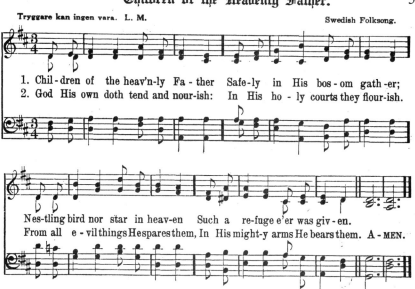

1. Chil-dren of the heav'n-ly Fa-ther Safe-ly in His bos-om gath-er;
2. God His own doth tend and nour-ish: In His ho-ly courts they flour-ish.

Nes-tling bird nor star in heav-en Such a re-fuge e'er was giv-en.
From all e-vil things He spares them, In His might-y arms He bears them. A-MEN.

3 Neither life nor death shall ever
From the Lord His children sever;
Unto them His grace He showeth,
And their sorrows all He knoweth.

4 Lo, their very hairs He numbers,
And no daily care encumbers
Them that share His every blessing,
And His help in woes distressing.

5 Praise the Lord in joyful numbers:
Your Protector never slumbers.
At the will of your Defender
Every foeman must surrender.

6 Though He giveth or He taketh,
God His children ne'er forsaketh,
His the loving purpose solely
To preserve them pure and holy.

Carolina Vilhelmina (Sandell) Berg, (1832-1903).

If a person from the Augustana tradition knows only one hymn in Swedish, it is *Tryggare kan ingen vara.* The words are by Lina Sandell-Berg (1832-1903), a leading hymn writer in the pietist revival in Sweden. For many years it was known only in Scandinavian circles, but now it is found in many hymnals. The tune probably came to Sweden via Germany. *The Hymnal* (1925) - No.487; *Service Book and Hymnal* (1958) - No.572; *Lutheran Book of Worship* (1978) - No.474

58   **Jesus Is My Joy, My All.**

Jesus allt mitt goda är. 7 8, 7 8, 7 7.   JAKOB ARRHENIUS? 1694.

1. Je - sus   is my Joy, my   All,   He   for   me His   life hath giv - en;
2. Rich-es, pomp, and earth-ly   joy   Can-not tempt my   soul from heav-en;

I am His, I hear His call;   He hath writ my name in heav - en.
Gold is min-gled with al - loy,   Bit.- ter - ness with sweet-ness giv - en,

Earth-ly treas-ures pass a - way;   Je - sus   I   will love for   aye.
Rich - es   flee and hopes de - cay;   Je - sus' grace a - bides al - way.   A - MEN.

3 In my Jesus I am blest,
    He to pleasant pastures leads me,
Stills my soul and gives it rest,
    And with heavenly manna feeds me.
Earthly things must fade and fall;
Jesus is my Life, my All.

4 Then away, O world! thy joy
    Leads the soul to grief and sorrow;
Death is found in sin's employ,
    Fears to-day, regrets to-morrow.
Jesus only satisfies;
Jesus points me to the skies!

Ahasuerus Fritsch. Johan Olof Wallin, 1814.

Archbishop Wallin translated this hymn by Ahasuerus Fritsch (1629-1701), chancellor of the University of Jena in Germany. He edited two hymn collections. The tune is linked with Jakob Arrhenius (1642-1725) a hymn writer who was professor of history at Uppsala University in Sweden.

The Hymnal (1925) - No.491

Nearer, Still Nearer, Close to Thy Heart.

Nearer, still nearer. 9 10, 9 10, 10.

MRS. C. H. MORRIS.

1. Near - er, still near - er, close to Thy heart, Draw me, my
2. Near - er, still near - er, noth - ing I bring, Naught as an

Sav - iour, so pre - cious Thou art; Fold me, O fold me
of - f'ring to Je - sus my King; On - ly my sin - ful,

close to Thy breast, Shel - ter me safe in that ha - ven of rest,
now con-trite heart, Grant me the cleans - ing Thy blood doth im - part,

Shel - ter me safe in that ha - ven of rest.
Grant me the cleans - ing Thy blood doth im - part. A - MEN.

Copyright, 1898, By H. L. Gilmour. Used by permission.

3 Nearer, still nearer, Lord, to be Thine,
Sin, with its follies, I gladly resign;
All of its pleasures, pomp, and its pride,
Give me but Jesus, my Lord crucified.

4 Nearer, still nearer, while life shall last,
Till safe in glory my anchor is cast;
Through endless ages ever to be,
Nearer, my Saviour, still nearer to Thee.

C. H. Morris.

One of the more than 1,000 gospel songs written by Leila Naylor Morris (1862-1929), a Methodist from Ohio who used the pen name, "Mrs. C. H. Morris." She wrote both the text and tune for this song which was popular both in churches and at camp meetings. *The Hymnal* (1925) - No.494

O Blessed Is the Man Who Stays.

Säll du, som dig åt Gud betror. 8 7, 8 7, 8 7, 8 7, 4 8.   BURKHARD WALDIS, 1553.

1. { O bless-ed is the man who stays His trust in God for-ev - er;
   { He dwells with-in the se-cret place Where foes may en-ter nev - er.

God is my Ref-uge and my Stay, My God who e'er di-rects me,

In dan-gers, fears, and plagues that slay, His wings shall still pro-tect me.

I will not fear When God, my Shield, is ev-er near. A-MEN.

2 Though thousands at my side may fall,
   Ten thousand near me stumble,
On Thee, my Saviour, will I call,
   Thou carest for the humble.
I will not fear the arrow's flight,
   Nor yet the dark night's terror:
Thy saints are precious in Thy sight,
   Thou keepest them from error,
For Thou hast sent
Thine angels bright to guard my tent.

3 "He loveth Me," thus saith the Lord,
   "Therefore will I uphold him;
Because he waits upon My Word,
   With love will I enfold him.
His enemies shall rage in vain,
   No evil shall come near him;
His prayers with Me acceptance gain,
   Before he calls, I'll hear him.
His days I'll bless
With joy, and peace, and righteousness."

91st Psalm, paraphrased by Ernest Edwin Ryden, 1924.
Based on Johan Olof Wallin's version.

A paraphrase of Psalm 91 by Ernest Edwin Ryden (1886-1981), hymn writer and editor of *The Lutheran Companion*. Dr. Ryden based his paraphrase on Johan Olof Wallin's version. The chorale melody is by Burkhard Waldis (c1490-1557), a German monk who became a Lutheran pastor and composer.

The Hymnal (1925) - No.495

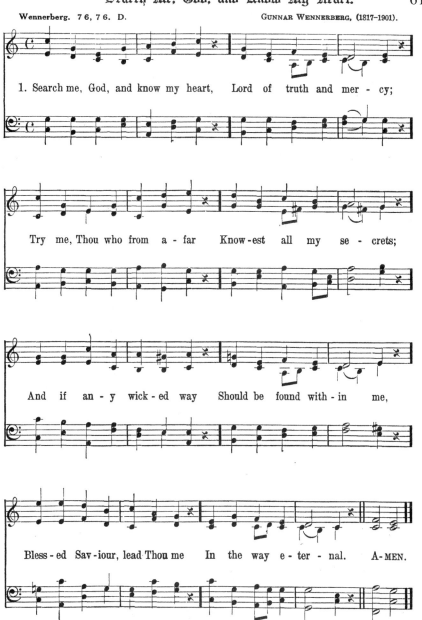

Search Me, God, and Know My Heart.

Wennerberg. 7 6, 7 6. D.   GUNNAR WENNERBERG, (1817-1901).

1. Search me, God, and know my heart, Lord of truth and mer - cy;

Try me, Thou who from a - far Know-est all my se - crets;

And if an - y wick - ed way Should be found with - in me,

Bless - ed Sav -iour, lead Thou me In the way e - ter - nal. A-MEN.

Ps. 139. 23, 24, paraphrased by Claus August Wendell, 1924.

Claus August Wendell (1866-1950), pastor of Grace Lutheran Church in Minneapolis for 34 years and an editor of *The Junior Hymnal*, wrote this paraphrase of Psalm 139:23-34. The tune, by Swedish composer Gunnar Wennerberg (1817-1901), is from his setting of this Psalm for solo voice, choir and piano accompaniment.   *The Hymnal* (1925) - No.496; *Service Book and Hymnal* (1958) - No.378; *Lutheran Book of Worship* (1978) - No.311

Day by Day Thy Mercies, Lord, Attend Me

Carolina V. (Sandell) Berg, (1832-1903)
Tr. Ernest Edwin Ryden, 1928

Oskar Ahnfelt, (1813-1882)

1. Day by day Thy mer - cies, Lord, at - tend me, O what
2. Thro' life's de - vious paths Thou e'er wilt guide me, For each
3. O what joy, be - neath Thy heav'n-ly fa - vor, Trust-ing-

com - fort in this hope to rest! All that Thou in love di - vine dost
need wilt give me plen-teous grace; In temp - ta-tion's storms wilt safe-ly
ly to rest my soul in Thee; Help me, Lord, that I may nev - er

send me, Draws me, Sav - iour, clos - er to Thy breast.
hide me, Till in glo - ry I be - hold Thy face.
wa - ver, Nor for - get Thy lov - ing care for me;

Thou dost love more ten - der - ly than ev - er Earth - ly
Thou hast prom - ised for each day and hour Grace to
For I know, no mat - ter what be - tide me, Thou wilt

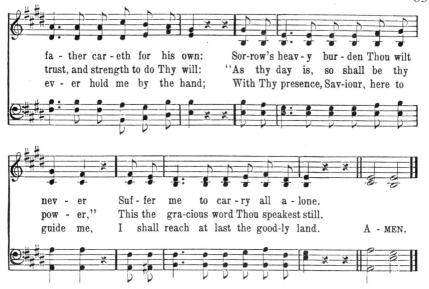

fa - ther car - eth for his own: Sor-row's heav-y bur - den Thou wilt
trust, and strength to do Thy will: "As thy day is, so shall be thy
ev - er hold me by the hand;   With Thy presence, Sav-iour, here to

nev - er   Suf-fer me to car-ry all a - lone.
pow - er,"   This the gra-cious word Thou speakest still.
guide me,   I shall reach at last the good-ly land.   A - MEN.

A well-known Swedish journalist has said that every Swede ought to begin each day with the song, "Blott
en dag ett ögonblick i sänder," (Day by day). Lina Sandell-Berg(1832-1903) wrote these words of comfort
and assurance. Oskar Ahnfelt (1832-1882) composed the tune especially for this hymn. It first appeared in
Andeliga Sånger in 1872 and was a favorite of many Swedish immigrants to the United States.

The Junior Hymnal (1928) - No.275

My Jesus, I Love Thee

Author Unknown

Adoniram J. Gordon, (1836-1895)

1. My Je - sus, I love Thee, I know Thou art mine,
2. I love Thee, be - cause Thou hast first lov - ed me,
3. In man - sions of glo - ry and end - less de - light,

For Thee all the fol - lies of sin I re - sign;
And pur - chased my par - don on Cal - va - ry's tree;
I'll ev - er a - dore Thee in heav - en so bright;

My gra - cious Re - deem - er, my Sav - iour art Thou;
I love Thee for wear - ing the thorns on Thy brow;
I'll sing with the glit - ter - ing crown on my brow,

If ev - er I loved Thee, my Je - sus, 'tis now. A-MEN.

A hymn tune by Adoniram Judson Gordon (1836-1895), a New England Baptist who founded Gordon College in Boston in 1889. Born in New Hampshire, Gordon also founded Clarenden Street Baptist Church in Boston. The text is by William R. Featherston, about whom nothing else is known.

The Junior Hymnal (1928) - No.22

I LIFT MY EYES. 9 8, 9 8.

RUDOLF LAGI, 1823–68

With movement

1. I lift my eyes un - to heaven a - bove, And fold my
2. How sweet to bless thee and praise thy Name, For thou, O

hands to draw near thee; For thou, dear Lord, dost thy
Christ, art my Sav - iour; Kind Shep - herd, guard me from

chil - dren love, And thou hast prom - ised to hear me.
sin and shame, And let me love thee for - ev - er.

3 A little flower in thy garden fair,
   My life to thee has been given;
  O Saviour, keep me in thy dear care,
   And bring me safely to heaven.

4 Dear Lord, I thank thee for all thy love
   And gifts divine beyond measure;
  A sweeter song I will raise above
   To thee, my heart's dearest treasure.

Johan Ludvig Runeberg, 1804–77
Tr. Hymnal Version, 1955

A much-loved children's hymn by Finland's national poet, Johan Ludvig Runeberg (1804-1877). Ernest E. Ryden (1886-1981) made the English paraphrase. The tune is by Rudolf Lagi (1823-1868), Finnish organist and composer.

Service Book and Hymnal (1978) - No.396

We've a Story to Tell to the Nations

Colin Sterne, 1896

H. Ernest Nichol, 1896

66

1. We've a sto - ry to tell to the na - tions, That shall
2. We've a song to be sung to the na - tions, That shall
3. We've a mes - sage to give to the na - tions, That the
4. We've a Sav - iour to show to the na - tions, Who the

turn their hearts to the right, A sto - ry of truth and sweet-ness,
lift their hearts to the Lord; A song that shall con - quer e - vil
Lord who reign - eth a - bove, Hath sent us His Son to save us,
path of sor - row has trod, That all of the world's great peo - ple

A sto - ry of peace and light, A sto - ry of peace and light.
And shat - ter the spear and sword, And shat - ter the spear and sword.
And show us that God is love, And show us that God is love.
Might come to the truth of God, Might come to the truth of God.

REFRAIN:

For the dark-ness shall turn to dawn - ing, And the dawn-ing to noon-day bright,

And Christ's great kingdom shall come on earth, The kingdom of love and light. A-MEN.

A vibrant missionary hymn which well expressed Augustana's strong foreign missions thrust. The text and tune are by Henry Ernest Nichol and first appeared in *The Sunday School Hymnary*, published in London in 1896. Some hymnals identify the composer of this hymn as "Colin Sterne", which is Nichol's pseudonym.

The Junior Hymnal (1928) - No.201

I'm a Pilgrim, and I'm a Stranger. 67

Jag är främling. 9 11, 10 10, 9 11.   OSKAR AHNFELT, (1813-1882).

1. I'm a pil-grim, and I'm a stran-ger, I can tar-ry, I can tar-ry but a night; Do not de-tain me, for I am go-ing To where the fountains are ev-er flow-ing: I'm a pil-grim, and I'm a stran-ger, I can tar-ry, I can tar-ry but a night. A - MEN.

2 There the glory is ever shining;
   O my longing heart, my longing heart is there:
   Here in this country so dark and dreary
   I long have wandered, forlorn and weary:
   I'm a pilgrim, and I'm a stranger,
   I can tarry, I can tarry but a night.

3 Of the city to which I'm going
   My Redeemer, my Redeemer is the light;
   There is no sorrow, nor any sighing,
   Nor any sinning, nor any dying:
   Of the city to which I'm going
   My Redeemer, my Redeemer is the light.

Mary S. B. Shindler, 1841.

Another favorite hymn by Oskar Ahnfelt (1813-1882), Swedish troubadour who toured his native land with a ten-string guitar during the the 19th century revival movement. The text by Mary Schindler (1810-1883) expresses the biblical image of our human lives as a pilgirmage.

Hymnal (1901) - No.338; *Söndagsskolbok* (1903) - No.151; *The Hymnal* (1925) - No.526

I Am Jesus' Little Lamb.

Weil ich Jesu Schäflein bin. 7 7, 8 8, 7 7.　　　　　　　　German.

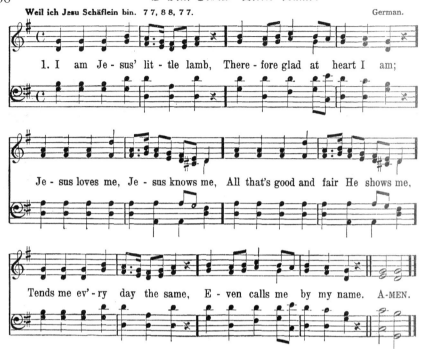

1. I am Je-sus' lit-tle lamb, There-fore glad at heart I am;

Je-sus loves me, Je-sus knows me, All that's good and fair He shows me,

Tends me ev'-ry day the same, E-ven calls me by my name. A-MEN.

2 Out and in I safely go,
   Want and hunger never know;
   Soft green pastures He discloseth,
   Where His happy flock reposeth;
   When I faint or thirsty be,
   To the brook He leadeth me.

3 Should not I be glad all day
   In this blessèd fold to stay,
   By this holy Shepherd tended,
   Whose kind arms, when life is ended,
   Bear me to the world of light?
   Yes, O yes, my lot is bright.

Henrietta Louise von Hayn. 1778.

A popular children's hymn sung at home and in Sunday School. Of German origin, it was much loved by the early Swedish immigrants. Henrietta Louisa von Hayn (1724-1782), a Moravian, wrote the words which are set to a traditional tune from Germany.

　　Hymnal (1901) - No.309; *Söndagsskolbok* (1903) - No.105; *The Hymnal* (1925) - No.650

Nun danket all' und bringet Ehr (Störl). C. M.   JOHANN GEORG CHRISTIAN STÖRL, 1710.

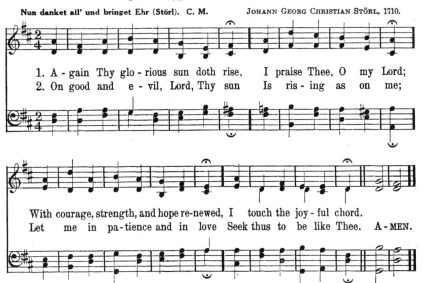

1. A - gain Thy glo - rious sun doth rise,   I praise Thee, O   my Lord;
2. On good and e - vil, Lord, Thy sun   Is ris - ing as   on   me;

With courage, strength, and hope re-newed, I   touch the joy - ful chord.
Let   me in pa - tience and in love Seek thus to be like Thee. A - MEN.

3 May I in virtue and in faith,
   And with Thy gifts content,
Rejoice beneath Thy covering wings,
   Each day in mercy sent.

4 Safe with Thy counsel in my work,
   Thee, Lord, I'll keep in view,
And feel that still Thy bounteous grace
   Is every morning new.
              Johan Olof Wallin, 1816.

classic morning hymn by Johan Olof Wallin (1779-1839), Sweden's most famous hymn writer, set to a
chorale tune by Johann Georg Christian Störl (1675-1719), German church musician who composed hymns
nd edited a hymn book.   *Hymnal* (1901) - No.170; *The Hymnal* (1925) - No.545

The Twilight Shadows Round Me Fall.

Cecile. C. M. D.

PETER JOHNSON, 1915.

1. The twi-light shad-ows round me fall, And night comes creep-ing on;

But Thou, dear Lord, art ev-er near, My Day when day is gone.

Thy wings in love o'er-shad-ow me, The night with Thee is light;

I rest in Thee, Thou Changeless One, And wait the dawning bright. A-MEN.

Or: Ishpeming, No. 557.

2 My life is but a fleeting day,
  My race, how quickly run!
The dawn and noonday glory fade
  Into the setting sun.
A stranger and a pilgrim here,
  With faltering feet I roam;
Lord, let Thy glory light the way
  That leads me to my home.

3 By faith I see the better land,
  Where falls no earthly night,
Where Thou dost shine, a radiant Sun,
  The Everlasting Light.
Then help me, Lord, to walk with Thee,
  And keep me Thine alway,
That when I sleep, I may awake
  Unto the perfect day.

Ernest Edwin Ryden, 1924.

An evening hymn by Ernest Edwin Ryden (1886-1981), Augustana Lutheran pastor, who wrote many hymns
plus translating others from Swedish and Finnish into English. He was editor of *The Lutheran Companion*
from 1934-1961. The melody is by Peter Johnson who was organist and choir director at Gustavus Adolphus
Lutheran Church in St Paul, Minnesota, from 1914-1945.

The Hymnal (1925) - No.556; *Service Book and Hymnal* (1958) - No.23

I Love to Steal Awhile Away.

Jag är så glad, när jag får gå. C. M.

SWEDISH FOLK MELODY.

1. I love to steal a-while a-way From ev-ery cum-bering care,

And spend the hours of set-ting day In hum-ble grate-ful prayer,

And spend the hours of set-ting day In hum-ble, grate-ful prayer. A-men.

2 I love in solitude to shed
   The penitential tear,
   And all His promises to plead
   Where none but God can hear.

3 I love to think of mercies past,
   And future good implore,
   And all my cares and sorrows cast
   On Him whom I adore.

4 I love by faith to take a view
   Of brighter scenes in heaven;
   The prospect doth my strength renew,
   While here by tempests driven.

5 Thus when life's toilsome day is o'er,
   May its departing ray
   Be calm as this impressive hour,
   And lead to endless day.

PHOEBE H. BROWN, (1783—1861), 1824.

A hymn by Phoebe Hinsdale Brown (1783-1861), considered American's first woman hymn writer. She wrote this "Twilight Hymn" in Massachusetts in 1818. It appeared in five Augustana hymnals. The tune used in the four earliest hymnals is a Swedish folk melody.   *Hemlandssånger* (1892) – No. 355;
Hymnal (1901) – No.180; *Söndagsskolbok* (1903) – No.127;
Lutherförbundets Sångbok (1913) – No.19; *The Hymnal* (1925) – No.555

72

Sun of My Soul, Thou Saviour Dear.

Hursley. L. M.

Attributed to PETER RITTER, 1792.

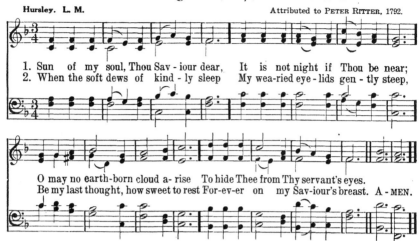

1. Sun of my soul, Thou Sav - iour dear, It is not night if Thou be near;
2. When the soft dews of kind - ly sleep My wea-ried eye - lids gen - tly steep,

O may no earth-born cloud a- rise To hide Thee from Thy servant's eyes.
Be my last thought, how sweet to rest For-ev-er on my Sav-iour's breast. A - MEN.

3 Abide with me from morn till eve,
For without Thee I cannot live;
Abide with me when night is nigh,
For without Thee I dare not die.

4 If some poor wandering child of Thine
Have spurned to-day the voice divine,
Now, Lord, the gracious work begin;
Let him no more lie down in sin.

5 Watch by the sick; enrich the poor
With blessings from Thy boundless store;
Be every mourner's sleep to-night,
Like infant's slumber, pure and light.

6 Come near and bless us when we wake,
Ere through the world our way we take;
Till in the ocean of Thy love
We lose ourselves in heaven above.

John Keble, 1827. a.

An English hymn by John Keble (1792-1866) which was included in all the English-language hymnals of the Augustana Church. Keble, a high church Anglican, wrote a devotional classic, *The Christian Year.* The melody is a form of "Grosser Gott," probably the best-known of all Roman Catholic hymn tunes.

Hymnal (1901) - No.173; *The Hymnal* (1925) - No.563; *Service Book and Hymnal* (1958) - No.226

Thy Holy Wings, Dear Savior

1 Thy ho - ly wings, dear Sav - ior, spread gen - tly o - ver me;
2 Thy par - don, Sav - ior, grant me, and cleanse me in thy blood;

and through the long night watch - es I'll rest se - cure in thee.
give me a will - ing spir - it, a heart both clean and good.

What - ev - er may be - tide me, be thou my hid - ing place,
O take in - to thy keep - ing thy chil - dren great and small,

and let me live and la - bor each day, Lord, by thy grace.
and while we sweet - ly slum - ber en - fold us' one and all. A - men.

WORDS: Lina Sandell, 1832-1903, tr. Ernest Edwin Ryden, 1886-1981, © Ernest Edwin Ryden
MUSIC: Swedish melody; arr. Mark S. Dickey, 1885-1961, © William K. Provine

7.6.7.6.D.
HOLY WINGS

A Swedish folk hymn with words by Lina Sandell-Berg (1832-1903) which has gained renewed popularity in recent years. Included in *Hemlandssånger* (Homeland Songs), it did not appear in later Augustana hymnals. Ernest E Ryden (1886-1981), one of Augustana's leading hymnists, provided the translation in the *Covenant Hymnal*.   *Hemlandssånger* (1892) - No.357

Jesus, Tender Shepherd, Hear Me.

Evening Prayer. 8 7, 8 7.

JOHN STAINER, 189

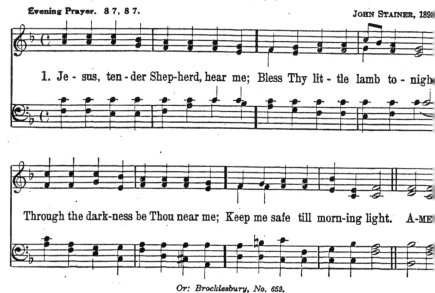

1. Je - sus, ten - der Shep-herd, hear me; Bless Thy lit - tle lamb to - nigh

Through the dark-ness be Thou near me; Keep me safe till morn-ing light. A-ME

Or: Brocklesbury, No. 659.

2 All this day Thy hand has led me,
   And I thank Thee for Thy care;
   Thou hast clothed me, warmed, and fed me,
   Listen to my evening prayer.

3 Let my sins be all forgiven;
   Bless the friends I love so well:
   Take me, Lord, at last to heaven,
   Happy there with Thee to dwell.

Mary (Lundie) Duncan. 1839

A children's hymn often used as a bedtime prayer. It appeared in *Rhymes for My Children* by Mary Lundie Duncan (1814-1840), wife of a Scottish Free Church minister from Britain. The tune is by John Stainer (1840-1901), a director of music at St Paul's Cathedral and later music professor at Oxford University
Hymnal (1901) - No.176; *The Hymnal* (1925) - No.661;
Service Book and Hymnal (1958) - No.235

In the Springtime Fair

In unison

1 In the spring-time fair but mor-tal, in the day of frag-ile flow'rs,
2 Though at ev-'ry mo-ment near you, is the Lord un-heed-ed still?

Christ is wait-ing at your por-tal, faith-ful through the pass-ing hours.
For how long will he con-tin-ue speak-ing to your shut-tered will?

Refrain

O-pen now, be-fore the au-tumn sweeps the sum-mer's flow'rs a-way;

o-pen while the sun is shin-ing— all too brief our earth-ly day!

WORDS: Lina Sandell, 1832-1903, tr. Karl A. Olsson, 1913-. © 1972, 1996 Covenant Publications
MUSIC: Swedish melody; arr. Norman E. Johnson, 1928-1983, © 1972, 1996 Covenant Publications

8.7.8.7. with Refrain
SPRINGTIME

Words copyright ©1972 1996. Reprinted by permission of Covenant Publications.

 hymn by Lina Sandell-Berg (1832-1903), a leading writer in the pietistic revival, which was sung in
wedish in Augustana congregations and was translated into English for use in the Mission Covenant
hurch. It is set to a lovely Swedish folk melody. *Hemlandssånger* (1892) - No.174;
Lutherförbundets Sångbok (1913) - No.95

Now Comes the Time for Flowers

1 Now comes the time for flow - ers, for joy, for beau - ty great.
2 Our love - ly flow - ered mead - ows, the tilled fields' no - ble seed,
3 We hear the bird - song ring - ing a man - y throat - ed laud:
4 You gen - tle Je - su, Chris - tus, our ra - diant sun, our shield,

Come near, you sum - mer hours, earth's grass - es re - cre - ate.
rich herbs laid out in wind - rows, green groves se - date - ly treed:
shall not our tongues be sing - ing our praise to Fa - ther God?
your light, your arm pro - tect us, to you cold sens - es yield.

Sun's kind and live - ly charm - ing of dead things win - ter slew,
these won - der - ful re - mind - ers of God's good King - dom strong;
My soul, lift up God's great - ness, a heart - y song em - ploy,
Bring fires of love in - tern - al, but damp the heats of lust,

comes in - ti - mate - ly warm - ing and all is born a - new!
that we his grace re - mem - ber, it spans the whole year long!
to him who wills to find us and bring us end - less joy.
pre - vent all hurt in - fer - nal: teach us your hand to trust.

WORDS: Israel Kolmodin, 1643-1709, tr. Zenos E. Hawkinson, 1925-, © 1978, 1996 Covenant Publications   7.6.7.6.D.
MUSIC: Swedish Koralbok, 1697   BLOMSTERTID
Words copyright ©1978, 1996. Reprinted by permission of Covenant Publications.

A classic Swedish hymn by Israel Kolmodin (1643-1709), Swedish Lutheran pastor and hymn writer. The melody appeared in the *Koralbok* of 1697 but is much older. Various texts are linked with this tune. We include the translation of the original hymn from the *Covenant Hymnal*.

Hymnal (1901) - No.168; *Söndagsskolbok* (1903) - No.211;
Service Book and Hymnal (1958) - No.449 (tune); *Lutheran Book of Worship* (1978) - No.515 (tune)

Summer Psalm

Waldemar Ahien
arr. Bertil E. Anderson

1. A frien — dly green does rich - ly dress each field and love — ly val — ley,
2. For for — tune and their sum-mer peace, The love — ly birds give praise.___
3. But you, O God, who made our world so love — ly in the sum — mer.

Now gen — tle bree — zes waft a — loft bird songs in roun - de - lay.___
From peace - ful nests in for — ests green, rings out their songs of grace.___
Give us your grace, your ho — ly word, your love to e — ver pon — der.

And sun's bright light, and peace - ful groves make sor — row's paths___ to
A hymn soars up___ with peace and hope from hearts so glad___ and
All flesh is grass; the flo - wers fade_ and time from all___ will

scat — ter, be — fore the ad — vent of sum — — mer.
free,___ From blos - soms and ___ from trees.___
se — ver. God's word re — mains___ for — e — — ver.

Bertil E. Anderson (1925-1993), an Augustana pastor and church musician, translated this lovely Swedish summer hymn which was included in *Hemlandssånger* (1892). The words are by Carl David af Wirsén (1842-1912), a member of the 1883 Swedish psalmbook committee. The tune now used is by Waldemar Åhlén (1894-1982), a church organist and composer from Stockholm.

Hemlandssånger (1892) - No.408

78   How Blessed Is This Place, O Lord.

Lob sei dem allmächtigen Gott. L. M.   JOHANN CRÜGER, 1640.

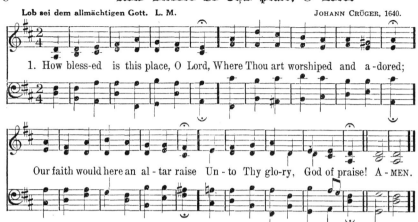

1. How bless-ed is this place, O Lord, Where Thou art worshiped and a-dored;

Our faith would here an al-tar raise Un-to Thy glo-ry, God of praise! A-MEN.

2 Here let Thy sacred fire of old
Descend to kindle spirits cold;
And may our prayers, when here we bend,
Like incense sweet to Thee ascend.

3 Here let the weary one find rest,·
The aching heart a comfort blest,
· The guilty soul a sure retreat,
The sinner pardon at Thy feet.

4 Here gather us around Thy board
To keep the feast with Thee, dear Lord,
And when in faith our souls draw near,
May we discern Thy presence here.

5 And when these earthly Sabbaths cease,
O may our souls depart in peace,
Around Thy glorious throne to meet,
And find it, Lord, a mercy-seat!

Ernest Edwin Ryden, 1924.

A hymn by Ernest Edwin Ryden (1886-1981), Augustana hymn writer and editor of *The Lutheran Companion*. He wrote this hymn for a church dedication, but it is suitable for other occasions. It has been set to various tunes. Here we use a German chorale melody by Johann Crüger (1598-1662)

The Hymnal (1925) - No.581;
Service Book and Hymnal (1958) - No.241; *Lutheran Book of Worship* (1978) - No.186

Lancashire. 7 6, 7 6. D. HENRY SMART, 1836.

1. O Lord, now let Thy serv-ant De-part with heav'n-ly peace,

For I have seen the glo - ry Of Thy re-deem-ing grace:

A Light to lead the Gen-tiles Un-to Thy ho-ly hill,

The glo-ry of Thy peo-ple, Thy cho-sen Is-ra-el. A-MEN.

2 How blessèd is the vision
  E'en here of Thy great love,
But still my spirit yearneth
  To see Thy face above,
Where in Thy holy image
  I, too, shall join the throng
Of ransomed souls in glory,
  And sing the Lamb's new song.

3 Then grant that I may follow
  Thy gleam, O glorious Light,
Till earthly shadows scatter,
  And faith is changed to sight;
Till raptured saints shall gather
  Upon that shining shore,
Where Christ, the blessèd Daystar,
  Shall light them evermore.

Ernest Edwin Ryden, 1924.

A paraphrase of the *Nunc Dimittis*, Simeon's song, by Ernest Edwin Ryden (1886-1981), Augustana pastor who was a hymn writer, author and editor. The Augustana hymnal of 1925 used a familiar tune by Henry Thomas Smart (1813-1879), an English musician and publisher.

The Hymnal (1925) - No.590; *Lutheran Book of Worship* (1978) - No.339

Lord Jesus Christ, True Man and God.

Misströsta ej att Gud är god. 8 8, 8 8, 8 8.

Swedish, 1695.
ISRAEL KOLMODIN? (1643-1709).

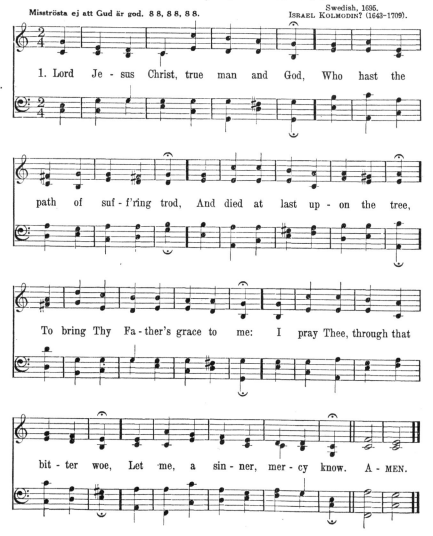

1. Lord Je - sus Christ, true man and God, Who hast the path of suf - f'ring trod, And died at last up - on the tree, To bring Thy Fa - ther's grace to me: I pray Thee, through that bit - ter woe, Let me, a sin - ner, mer - cy know. A - MEN.

2 When comes the hour of failing breath,
And I must wrestle, Lord, with death,
Then come, Lord Jesus, come with speed,
And help me in my hour of need;
Lead me from this dark vale beneath,
And shorten Thou the pangs of death.

Paul Eber, 1565.

A hymn of the Reformation period by Paul Eber (1511-1569) who was assistant to Philip Melanchthon at Wittenberg University in Germany. Israel Kolmodin (1643-1709), Swedish Lutheran pastor and hymn writer, composed the tune.   *Hymnal* (1901) - No.320; *The Hymnal* (1925) - No.594

I hoppet sig min frälsta själ förnöjer. 11 11, 5 5 11.   Northern Melody from 16th Century.

1. { In   hope my   soul, re-deemed to   bliss un - end - ing, }
   { To   heav-en's glo-rious height by   faith as - cend - ing, }

Is   mind-ful ev - er   That Christ did sev - er

The bonds of death, that I might live for-ev - er.   A - MEN.

2 In Him I have salvation's way discovered,
  The heritage for me He hath recovered.
        Though death o'ertakes me,
        Christ ne'er forsakes me,
  To everlasting life He surely wakes me.

3 More radiant there than sun e'er shone in brightness,
  My soul shall shine before God's throne in whiteness.
        My God, who knows me,
        In glory clothes me,
  As He declared when for His own He chose me.

4 O may I come where strife and grief are ended,
  Where all Thy saints shall meet, with peace attended!
        Lord, grant Thy favor
        And mercy ever,
  And turn my sorrow into joy forever.

5 Lord Jesus Christ, keep me prepared and waking,
  Till from the vale of tears Thy bride Thou'rt taking
        To dwell in heaven,
        Where joy is given,
  And clouds of darkness are forever riven.

Elle Andersdatter, 1645?

A funeral hymn by Elle Andersdatter (died 1643), a Danish housewife, which was edited by Johan Olof Wallin (1779-1839). It appeared in the 1819 Swedish *Koralbok*. The source of the tune is unknown other than it came from the North and goes back at least to the 16th century.

Hymnal (1901) - No.326; *The Hymnal* (1925) - No.602

I Near the Grave, Where'er I Go.

Jag går mot döden, hvar jag går. 8 7, 8 7, 6 6, 8 8.

Cantional Gotha, 1726.

1. I near the grave, wher-e'er I go, Wher-e'er my path-way tend - eth;

If rough or pleas-ant here be - low, My way at death's gate end - eth.

I have no oth - er choice; Be - tween my griefs and joys My mor-tal

life is or-dered so: I near the grave, wher-e'er I go. A - MEN.

2 I go to heaven, where'er I go,
    If Jesus' steps I follow;
The crown of life He will bestow,
    When earth this frame shall swallow.
    If through this tearful vale
    I in that course prevail,
And walk with Jesus here below,
    I go to heaven, where'er I go.

Hans Adolph Brorson, 1734.

A hymn reminding us of our mortality and the gift of life eternal by Hans Adolf Brorson (1694-1764), a bishop who was one of Denmark's finest hymn writers. The 18th century tune is from Gotha (southern Sweden). *The Hymnal* (1925) - No.603

Daystar. 7 6, 7 6. D.

SAMUEL MARTIN MILLER, 1922.
Harmonized by GERHARD THEODORE ALEXIS, 1925.

1. When Je-sus comes in glo-ry, As Lord and King of kings,
2. His voice like rush-ing wa-ters Will reach with might-y sound

O what a won-drous sto-ry The bless-ed Bi-ble brings:
In-to the deep-est quar-ters Of all cre-a-tion round;

His face will shine like sun-light, His head be white as snow,
And at this won-drous greet-ing The dead in Christ shall rise,

His eyes like flam-ing fire-light, His feet like brass a-glow.
Their Lord and Sav-iour meet-ing In glo-ry in the skies. A-MEN.

3 And we who are believing,
  And His appearing love,
Shall know we are receiving
  His glory from above;
His resurrection power
  Will raise us to the place
Where we that wondrous hour
  Shall see Him face to face.

4 O hasten Thine appearing,
  Thou Bright and Morning Star!
Lord, may we soon be hearing
  The trumpet sound afar;
Thy people all are yearning
  To be Thy raptured bride,
And at Thine own returning
  Be caught up to Thy side.

Samuel Martin Miller. 1922.

A hymn about Christ's second coming by Samuel Martin Miller (1890-1975), an Augustana pastor who was dean of the Lutheran Bible Institute in Minneapolis from 1919-1931 and again from 1935-1945. Gerhard Theodore Alexis (1889-1927), an Augustana church musician, harmonized Miller's tune for the hymn.
The Hymnal (1925) - No.615; *The Junior Hymnal* (1928) - No.285

84

There's a Land That Is Fairer Than Day.

Sweet by and by. 9 9, 9 9. With Refrain.

JOSEPH PHILBRICK WEBSTER, 1868.

By permission of Oliver Ditson Co., owners of copyright.

2 We shall sing on that beautiful shore
  The melodious songs of the blest,
And our spirits shall sorrow no more,
  Not a sigh for the blessing of rest.

3 To our bountiful Father above
  We will offer our tribute of praise
For the glorious gift of His love,
  And the blessings that hallow our days.

S. Fillmore Bennett.

A Gospel hymn by Sanford Fillmore Bennett (1836-1898), an educator and medical doctor who spent many years in Elkhorn, Wisconsin. The tune is by Joseph Philbrick Webster (1819-1874), a prolific composer of popular music who was born in New York but lived the last 16 years of his life in Elkhorn, Wisconsin. *The Hymnal* (1925) - No.621; *Junior Hymnal* (1928) – No.295

I himmelen, i himmelen. 86, 86, 886.

Koralbok, 1697.

1. In heav'n a - bove, in heav'n a - bove, Where God our Fa - ther dwells:
2. In heav'n a - bove, in heav'n a - bove, What glo - ry deep and bright!

How bound - less there the bless - ed - ness! No tongue its great - ness
The splen - dor of the noon - day sun Grows pale be - fore its

tells: There face to face, and full and free, Ev - er and
light: The might - y Sun that ne'er goes down, A - round whose

ev - er - more we see— We see the Lord of hosts!
gleam clouds nev - er frown, Is God the Lord of hosts. A - MEN.

3 In heaven above, in heaven above,
   No tears of pain are shed:
There nothing e'er shall fade or die;
   Life's fullness round is spread,
And, like an ocean, joy o'erflows,
   And with immortal mercy glows
     Our God the Lord of hosts.

4 In heaven above, in heaven above,
   God hath a joy prepared,
Which mortal ear hath never heard,
   Nor mortal vision shared,
Which never entered mortal breast,
   By mortal lips was ne'er expressed,
     O God the Lord of hosts!

Johan Åström, 1819.

...haps the most often-used funeral hymn in the Augustana Church. The text was written by a Swedish
...tor, Laurentius Laurentii Laurinus (1573-1655), for his wife's funeral in 1620. Two centuries later, Johan
...rom (1767-1844), another Swedish pastor, revised the text. Augustana used a tune from the Swedish
...*ralbok* of 1697 rather than the Norwegian folk melody often used today. *The Hymnal* (1925) - No.628;
       Service Book and Hymnal (1958) - No.146; *Lutheran Book of Worship* (1978) - No.330

There Are Treasures for Children in Heaven Above

From the Swedish
Tr. Ernest Edwin Ryden, 1927

Composer Unknown

1. There are treas-ures for chil-dren in heav-en a-bove, For the
2. They shall drink of the riv-er that flows from the throne, They shall
3. They shall join in the an-thems of glo-ry and praise, They shall

chil-dren who trust in their Lord; They shall dwell in the light of His
feast with the ran-somed and blest, They shall tell of His glo-ry who
sing with the an-gels so fair; And no sor-row or sigh-ing shall

fa - vor and love, They shall praise Him with joy-ous ac - cord.
calls them His own In that beau-ti-ful coun-try of rest.
hush their sweet lays, When they meet their Re-deem-er up there.

REFRAIN:

There are treas-ures in heav'n, there are treas-ures in heav'n, There are

treas-ures for chil-dren in heav'n; In the man-sions so bright, Where the

Lord is the Light, Shall the treas-ures to chil-dren be giv'n. A-MEN.

A children's hymn translated from the Swedish by Ernest Edwin Ryden (1886-1981). The author and composer are not known. *The Junior Hymnal* (1928) - No.287

When He Cometh, When He Cometh.

When He cometh. 8 6, 8 5. With Refrain.

GEORGE FREDERICK ROOT, 1866.

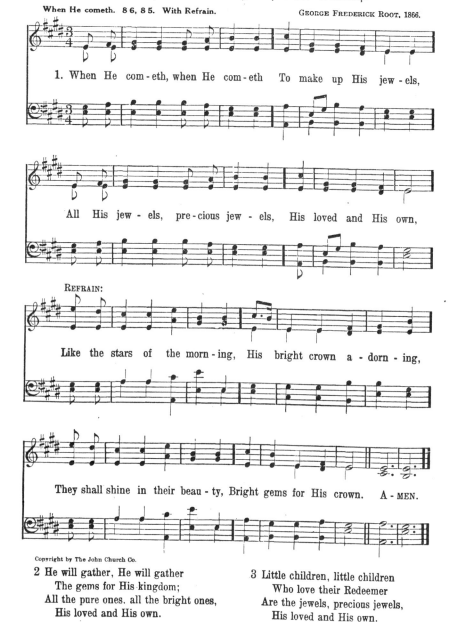

1. When He com-eth, when He com-eth To make up His jew-els,

All His jew-els, pre-cious jew-els, His loved and His own,

REFRAIN:

Like the stars of the morn-ing, His bright crown a-dorn-ing,

They shall shine in their beau-ty, Bright gems for His crown. A-MEN.

Copyright by The John Church Co.

2 He will gather, He will gather
  The gems for His kingdom;
All the pure ones, all the bright ones,
  His loved and His own.

3 Little children, little children
  Who love their Redeemer
Are the jewels, precious jewels,
  His loved and His own.

William Orcutt Cushing. (1823—).

A popular children's hymn by William Orcutt Cushing (1823-1902), a pastor who served churches in various parts of New York State. He wrote over 300 hymns, most of them during his retirement. The tune is by George Frederick Root (1820-1895), an organist in churches in Boston, New York and Chicago.

The Hymnal (1925) - No.651; *The Junior Hymnal* (1928) - No.286.

The Service

Advent, Christmas, and Epiphany Seasons.

OSKAR LINDBERG.

Lenten Season.

OSCAR BLOM.

Ho - ly, Ho - ly, Ho - - ly is the Lord .... of Hosts! The whole earth is full of His glo - - ry.

Ho - ly, Ho - - ly, Ho - ly is the Lord of Hosts! The whole earth is full of His glo - - ry.

HARALD FRYKLÖF.

Ho - ly, Ho - ly, Ho - ly is the Lord of Hosts!

The whole earth . . . is full of His glo - - ry.

Trinity Season.*

Ho - ly, Ho - ly, Ho - ly is the Lord of Hosts!

The whole earth . . . is full of His glo - - ry.

* Melody and tenor may be sung as a duet.

The Lord is in His holy temple; His throne is in heaven. The Lord is nigh unto them that are of an humble and contrite spirit. He heareth the supplications of the penitent and inclineth to their prayers. Let us therefore draw near with boldness unto His throne of grace and confess our sins:

The Confession of Sins

The **Minister** *shall turn to the Altar, and with the* **Congregation** *unite in the following Confession of Sins:*

Holy and righteous God, merciful Father, we confess unto Thee that we are by nature sinful and unclean, and that we have sinned against Thee by thought, word, and deed. We have not loved Thee above all things, nor our neighbor as ourselves, and are worthy, therefore, to be cast away from Thy presence if Thou shouldst judge us according to our sins. But Thou hast promised, O heavenly Father, to receive with tender mercy all penitent sinners who turn unto Thee and with a living faith seek refuge in Thy Fatherly compassion and in the merits of the Saviour, Jesus Christ. Their transgressions Thou wilt not regard, nor impute unto them their sins. Relying upon Thy promise, we confidently beseech Thee to be merciful and gracious unto us and to forgive us all our sins, to the praise and glory of Thy Holy Name.

May the Almighty, Eternal God, in His infinite mercy and for the sake of our Saviour, Jesus Christ, forgive all our sins, and give us grace to amend our lives, and with Him obtain eternal life. Amen.

Or, the following may be used during Lent and on Holy Days:

Have mercy upon me, O God, according to Thy lovingkindness: according to the multitude of Thy tender mercies blot out my transgressions. Wash me thoroughly from mine iniquity, and cleanse me from my sin. For I know my transgressions; and my sin is ever before me. Against Thee, Thee only, have I sinned, and done that which is evil in Thy sight. Hide Thy face from my sins, and blot out all mine iniquities. Create in me a clean heart, O God; and renew a right spirit within me. Cast me not away from Thy presence; and take not Thy Holy Spirit from me.

Heavenly Father, hear my prayer for the sake of Thy Son, Jesus Christ. Amen.

The **Minister** *and the* **Congregation** *shall rise and sing:*

Advent, Christmas, and Epiphany Seasons.

I.

Nürnberger Agende, 1639.

Lord, ... have mer - cy up - on us!

Christ, ... have mer - cy up - on us!

Lord, ... have mer - cy up - on us! . . . .

Modulation to Gloria in D, p. 96

II.

From FELTON.

Lord, have mer - cy up - on us! Christ, have mer - cy

up - on us! Lord, have mer - cy up - on us!

Lenten Season.

Bohemian Brethren, 1556.

Lord, ... have mer - cy up - on us! . . . .

Christ, ... have mer - cy up - on us! . . . .

Lord, ... have mer - cy up-on us! . . . .

Modulation to
Gloria in F, p. 96

Trinity Season. May also be used during *Lenten Season.*

I.   Bjuråkers Handskrift, prior to 1550.

Lord, ... have mer - - - - cy up-on us!   *Modulation to Gloria in F, p. 568.*

II.   GERHARD THEODORE ALEXIS, 1925.

Lord, . . . have mer - cy up - on us!   Christ, ... have

mer - cy up - on us! . . . . . . Lord, . . . have mer - cy

up - on us! . . . . .   *Modulation to Gloria in F, p. 96.*

The Minister, still turned to the Congregation, shall sing or say:

NICOLAUS DECIUS ? 1539.

All glo - ry be to Thee, Most High, To Thee all ad - o-

ra - tion! In grace and truth Thou draw - est nigh To of - fer

us sal - va - tion. Thou show - est Thy good will to

men, And peace shall reign on earth a - gain; We praise Thy

Name for - ev - er. *Modulation to B♭.*   *Modulation to G minor. (Lent.)*

Glory be to   God on high,   and on earth   peace, good will toward men.
{We praise Thee,} wor-ship Thee, {we glorify Thee,} Thee for Thy great glory.
{we bless Thee, we}   {we give thanks to}

O Lord God,   Heav'n-ly King,   God the   Fa - ther Al - - mighty.
{O Lord, the Only-} Je - sus Christ; {O Lord God,} Son   of the Father,
{ begotten Son, }   {Lamb of God,}

That takest away.. the   sin.. of the world,   have mercy up - on   us.
Thou that takest away.. the   sin.. of the world,   re - - - ceive our prayer.
{ Thou that sittest } God the   Father, have mercy up - on   us.
{at the right hand.. of}

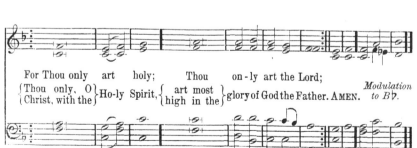

For Thou only   art   holy;   Thou   on-ly art the Lord;
{Thou only, O} Ho-ly Spirit, { art most } glory of God the Father. AMEN.
{Christ, with the}   {high in the}

Modulation to B♭.

Then the Minister shall turn to the Congregation and sing or say:

The Congregation shall sing:

The Lord be with you.

And with thy spir - it.

Lenten Season

The Minister:

The Congregation:

The Lord be with you.

And with thy spir - it.

Then the Minister shall say:

Let us pray.

The Collect

The Minister, turning to the Altar, shall read on Sundays and Festival Days the proper Collect. On special occasions one of the following may be used:

O Lord God, Heavenly Father, Thou Who hast no pleasure in the death of the wicked, but that they turn from their way and live: we pray Thee that Thou wouldst mercifully avert the punishment that our sins deserve, for the sake of Jesus Christ, our Lord.

Or:

We beseech Thee, Almighty God, Heavenly Father, to grant us a true faith, a firm hope in Thy mercy, and a sincere love to our fellow men, through Jesus Christ, our Lord.

The Congregation shall sing:

Lenten Season.

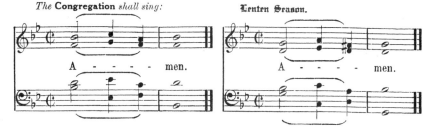

A - - - men.

A - - - men.

The Minister shall turn to the Congregation and say:

The Epistle for (*here he shall name the Sunday or Festival Day*) is written in . . . .

The Epistle ended, the Minister shall turn to the Altar, and the Congregation shall be seated. A Hymn (The Gradual) shall then be sung.

The Gospel

The Hymn ended, the Minister shall turn to the Congregation and say:

Lift up your hearts unto the Lord and hear the Gospel for the Day as it is written in . . . . . .

The Congregation shall arise, and the Gospel for the Day shall be read. The Gospel ended, the Minister and the Congregation shall say

The Apostles' Creed

I believe in God the Father Almighty, Maker of heaven and earth;

And in Jesus Christ His only Son, our Lord: Who was conceived by the Holy Spirit, Born of the Virgin Mary; Suffered under Pontius Pilate, Was crucified, dead and buried; He descended into hell; The third day He rose again from the dead; He ascended into heaven, And sitteth on the right hand of God the Father Almighty; From thence He shall come to judge the quick and the dead.

I believe in the Holy Spirit; The Holy Christian Church, the Communion of saints; The Forgiveness of sins; The Resurrection of the body; And the Life everlasting. Amen.

Or:

The Nicene Creed

I believe in one God, the Father Almighty, Maker of heaven and earth, And of all things visible and invisible;

And in one Lord Jesus Christ, the Only-begotten Son of God, Begotten of His Father before all worlds, God of God, Light of Light, Very God of Very God, Begotten, not made, Being of one substance with the Father, By Whom all things were made; Who, for us men, and for our salvation, came down from heaven, and was incarnate by the Holy Spirit of the Virgin Mary, and was made man; and was crucified also for us under Pontius Pilate. He suffered and was buried; And the third day He rose again, according to the Scriptures; And ascended into heaven, and sitteth on the right hand of the Father; And He shall come again with glory to judge both the quick and the dead; Whose kingdom shall have no end.

And I believe in the Holy Spirit, the Lord and Giver of Life, Who proceedeth from the Father and the Son, Who with the Father and the Son together is worshiped and glorified, Who spake by the Prophets.

And I believe in one holy Christian and Apostolic Church.

I acknowledge one Baptism for the remission of sins; and I look for the resurrection of the dead; and the life of the world to come. Amen.

*An **Anthem** in harmony with the lessons for the day may here be sung. Then shall follow one or more verses of a **Hymn** as an introduction to the Sermon. In the meantime the **Minister** shall enter the Pulpit.*

The Sermon

*The Sermon ended, the **Minister** shall offer a prayer in his own words or the following:*

Praised be the Lord, and blessed forever, Who by His Word has comforted, taught, exhorted, and admonished us. May His Holy Spirit confirm the Word in our hearts, that we be not forgetful hearers, but daily increase in faith, hope, love, and patience unto the end, and obtain salvation through Jesus Christ our Lord. Amen.

Here may be used the prayer to be found in the lectionary of the pastor's altar book after the texts of each Sunday.

*The **Church Notices** may then be given. The **Announcement of a Death** within the Congregation may be made as follows:*

We are again reminded that here we have no abiding city. It has pleased the Lord in His infinite wisdom to call from our midst N. N. at the age of ......

The Lord teach us so to consider our own departure, that when the hour is come we may be prepared for a blessed entrance into the heavenly kingdom.

*When **Intercession for the Sick** is requested, the **Minister** shall say:*

N. N. and N. N., who are sick, desire to be remembered in the prayers of the Congregation:

Almighty and Eternal God, Thou art the health and strength of them that trust in Thee. We pray Thee that Thou wouldst look in mercy upon the sick and the needy, and especially upon Thy servants for whom we now invoke Thy mighty aid. Turn their distress unto good, and if it be Thy will restore them to health. But above all give them healing for the soul through Thy holy Word. Help them by the remembrance of the bitter passion of Thy Son patiently to bear the affliction with which Thou hast visited them. And finally, when their hour is come, deliver them from all evil and bring them safe to Thy heavenly kingdom; through Thy Son, Jesus Christ, our Lord. Amen.

The grace of the Lord Jesus Christ, and the love of God, and the communion of the Holy Spirit, be with you all. Amen. (2 Cor. 13. 14.)

Or:

The God of all grace, Who called you unto His eternal glory in Christ, after that ye have suffered a little while, shall Himself perfect, establish, strengthen you. To Him be the dominion for ever and ever. Amen. (1 Pet. 5. 10, 11).

Easter and Pentecost Seasons.

Now the God of Peace, Who brought again from the dead the great Shepherd of the sheep with the blood of an eternal covenant, even our Lord Jesus, make you perfect in every good thing to do His will, working in us that which is well pleasing in His sight, through Jesus Christ; to whom be the glory for ever and ever. Amen. (Heb. 13. 20, 21.)

Trinity Season.

Now unto Him that is able to do exceeding abundantly above all that we ask or think, according to the power that worketh in us, unto Him be the glory in the Church and in Christ Jesus unto all generations for ever and ever. Amen. (Eph. 3. 20, 21).

At the End of the Church Year.

The God of peace Himself sanctify you wholly; and may your spirit and soul and body be preserved entire, without blame at the coming of our Lord Jesus Christ. Amen. (1 Th. 5. 23).

The Offering

Then shall an **Offertory** *be played, or an* **Anthem** *sung, during which the* **Offering** *shall be made. The* **Minister,** *having received the offering, shall place it upon the Altar and pray as follows:*

O God, Thou Giver of all good gifts, graciously receive and bless this offering which we Thy people place upon Thine Altar, for Jesus' sake. Amen.*

Then shall the **Congregation** *sing a* **Hymn,** *during which the* **Minister** *shall proceed to the Altar.*

The Salutation

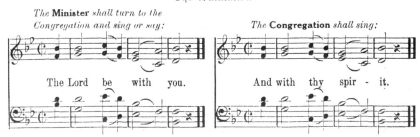

The **Minister** *shall turn to the Congregation and sing or say:*

The Lord be with you.

The **Congregation** *shall sing:*

And with thy spir - it.

* A short offertory sentence may then be sung by the Choir.

The **Minister:** — The Lord be with you.

The **Congregation:** — And with thy spir-it.

The **Minister** *shall say:*

Let us pray.

Turning to the Altar, the **Minister** *shall offer*

The General Prayer*

Almighty and most Merciful God, the Father of our Lord Jesus Christ: We give Thee thanks for all Thy goodness and tender mercies. Be gracious unto us and remember not our sins. Sanctify and guide us through Thy Holy Spirit, and grant that we may walk in holiness of life according to Thy Word. Unite, strengthen, and preserve Thy Church through the Word and the Holy Sacraments. Have mercy, O Lord, on all the nations that walk in darkness and that dwell in the land of the shadow of death, and cause the saving and life-giving light of Thy Gospel to shine graciously upon them.

For Synodical and Conference Meetings. Bless those who are now assembled to deliberate concerning the welfare of Thy Church, that their counsels may further Thy glory and the upbuilding of Thy kingdom among us.

Be Thou the strength and stay of our land. Give it grace and honor. Grant health and prosperity to all in authority, especially to the President (and the Congress) of the United States, the Governor (and the Legislature) of this Commonwealth, and to all our Judges and Magistrates. Endue them with grace to rule after Thy good pleasure, to the maintenance of righteousness, and to the hindrance and punishment of wickedness, that we may lead a quiet and peaceable life in all godliness and honesty.

---

*On special Festival Days the prayers prescribed should precede the General Intercession. According to circumstances, those parts of the General Intercession referring to conditions that do not always prevail are omitted, such as the prayers for Church assemblies, for Confirmation Candidates, etc. Occasional prayers shall, when they occur, follow the General Prayer. During Lent and on special occasions the Litany may be used instead of the General Prayer.

Help us, O God, that we may live together in peace and concord, with true and Christian counsel in all that we undertake. Prosper every good work, and turn away from us all harm and evil. May Thy blessing rest upon the fruits of the earth, and give success to every lawful occupation on land and sea.

Let the light of Thy Word ever shine within our homes. Keep the children of the Church in the covenant which Thou hast made with them in Holy Baptism, and give all parents and teachers grace to nurture them in Thy truth and fear. Bless, we pray Thee, the institutions of the Church: its colleges, its seminaries, and all its schools; that they may send forth men and women to serve Thee, in the Ministry of the Word, the Ministry of Mercy, and all the walks of life.

For Catechumens. Regard with special favor those who are being prepared for their first communion. Illumine their hearts and minds, and grant them unfeigned faith that they may ever walk as Thy disciples in the way of truth.

Help and comfort the sick and the poor, the oppressed and those who mourn, the afflicted and the dying. Graciously protect all widows and orphans. Support us in our last hour, and after this transitory life vouchsafe unto us eternal blessedness: through Jesus Christ, our Lord.

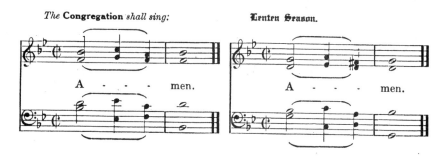

When Holy Communion is celebrated, the Lord's Prayer is omitted here. For The Service without Holy Communion, the Lord's Prayer is included here, followed by the Benedicamus (Page 112)

The Lord's Prayer

*The **Minister** together with the **Congregation** shall continue:*

Our Father, Who art in heaven: Hallowed be Thy Name; Thy kingdom come; Thy will be done on earth, as it is in heaven; Give us this day our daily bread; and forgive our trespasses, as we forgive those who trespass against us; And lead us not into temptation; but deliver us from evil; For Thine is the kingdom, and the power, and the glory, forever. Amen.

O Lamb of God, Most Holy

Then the **Congregation** *shall sing.* **"O Lamb of God, Most Holy,"** *while the* **Minister** *makes ready the elements of the Sacrament on the Altar.*

NIKOLAUS DECIUS, 1539.

O Lamb of God, most ho - ly, On Cal - va - ry an of - f'ring;

De - spis - ed, meek, and low - ly, Thou in Thy death and suf - f'ring

Our sins didst bear, our an - guish; The might of death didst van - quish;

Give us Thy peace, O Je - sus!   I. *Modulation to E♭.*   II. *Modulation to G minor.*

106

The Preface

I. *The Minister shall turn to the Congregation and sing or say:*

Lift up your hearts unto God.

The Congregation shall sing:

We lift them up un-to the Lord our God.

II. *The Minister:*

Lift up your hearts un-to God.

The Congregation:

We lift them up unto the Lord our God.

I. *The Minister shall sing or say:*

Let us give thanks un-to the Lord.

The Congregation shall sing:

It is meet and right so to do.

II. *The Minister:*

Let us give thanks unto the Lord.

The Congregation:

It is meet and right so to do.

Vere Dignum

The Minister shall turn to the Altar and say:

It is truly meet, right, and salutary, that we should at all times, and in all places, give thanks unto Thee, O Lord, Holy Father, Almighty, Everlasting God, through Jesus Christ, our Lord. He is our Paschal Lamb, offered for us, the innocent Lamb of God, that taketh away the sin of the world. As He hath conquered death, is risen again, and liveth for evermore, even so all they who put their trust in Him shall through Him be victorious over sin and death, and inherit eternal life. And in order that we may keep in remembrance His unspeakable mercy, He hath instituted His Holy Supper.

---

* The setting chosen (I. or II.) shall be followed consistently throughout the service.

Then shall the **Minister** *say:*

Our Lord Jesus Christ, in the night in which He was betrayed, took bread; and when He had given thanks, He brake it and gave it to His disciples, saying, Take, eat; this is My Body, which is given for you; this do in remembrance of Me.

After the same manner, also, when He had supped, He took the cup, and when He had given thanks, He gave it to them, saying, Drink ye all of it; this Cup is the New Testament in My Blood, which is shed for you, and for many, for the remission of sins; this do, as oft as ye drink it, in remembrance of Me.

The Lord's Prayer

The **Minister,** *together with the* **Congregation,** *shall say:*

Our Father, Who art in heaven; Hallowed be Thy Name; Thy kingdom come; Thy will be done on earth, as it is in heaven; Give us this day our daily bread; And forgive us our trespasses, as we forgive those who trespass against us; And lead us not into temptation; But deliver us from evil; For Thine is the kingdom, and the power, and the glory, forever. Amen.

Sanctus

Then shall the **Minister** *and the* **Congregation** *together sing:*

Ho - ly, Ho - ly, Ho - - ly, Lord God Al-might-y; Heav'n and earth are full of Thy glo - - ry; Ho - san-na in the high - est. Bless-ed is He that com-eth in the Name of the Lord. Ho - san-na in the high - est.

II.

Ho - ly, Ho - ly, Ho - ly, Lord God Al - might - y;

Heav'n and earth are full of Thy glo - ry; Ho-

san - na in the high - est. Bless - ed is He that com - eth

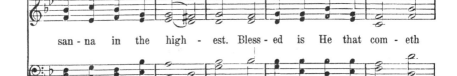

in the Name of the Lord. Ho - san-na in the high - est.

Pax

The **Minister,** *turning to the Congregation, shall sing or say:*

I.

The peace of the Lord be with you al - way. *Modulation to F minor.*

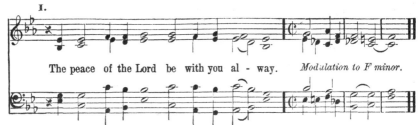

The peace of the Lord be with you al - way.

Agnus Dei

The Communicants now come forward while the **Congregation** *sings:*

O Lamb of God, That tak-est a-way the sin of the world; Save us, mer-ci-ful Lord God! O Lamb of God, That tak-est a-way the sin of the world; Hear us, mer-ci-ful Lord God! O Lamb of God, That tak-est a-way the sin of the world, Give us Thy peace and bless - ing. . . . .

110

II.

O Lamb of God, That tak-est a-way the sin of the world; Save us,

mer-ci-ful Lord God! O Lamb of God, That tak-est a-way the sin of the

world; Hear us, mer-ci-ful Lord God! O Lamb of God, That tak-est a-

way the sin of the world, Give us Thy peace and bless - ing.

During the distribution, appropriate **Hymns** *are sung by the* **Congregation,** *with subdued organ accompaniment. The* **Minister** *first administers the* **Bread** *to each communicant with these words:**

The Body of Christ given for thee.

And then the **Cup** *with these words:*

The Blood of Christ shed for thee.

To each group of communicants, as they leave the communion table, the **Minister** *says:*

The Lord Jesus Christ, Whose Body and Blood ye have now received, preserve you unto everlasting life. Amen.

* When the officiating Pastor administers communion to himself he shall, when the first group of communicants have knelt at the chancel, kneel at the Altar and administer the bread to himself with the words: "The Body of Christ given for me." He shall then rise and administer to the kneeling communicants. In the distribution of the wine he proceeds in the same manner with the words: "The Blood of Christ shed for me." At the final salutation to this group of communicants the words "we" and "us" should be substituted for "ye" and "you." When two Ministers are officiating they may first administer to each other before the Altar.

Jesus Christ, Whose Body thou now receivest, preserve thee unto everlasting life.

And at the administration of the **Cup:**

Jesus Christ, Whose Blood thou now receivest, preserve thee unto everlasting life.

In dismissing the communicants the **Minister** *shall say:*

The Grace and Peace of our Lord Jesus Christ be with you all. Amen.

The Thanksgiving

When the distribution is ended, the **Minister** *shall say:*

Let us pray.

The **Congregation** *shall rise. Turning to the Altar, the* **Minister** *shall say:*

We thank Thee, Almighty Father, Who, through Thy Son Jesus Christ, for our consolation and salvation hast instituted this Holy Supper: we pray Thee, grant us grace so to commemorate the death of Christ that we may be partakers of the great Supper in heaven.

Or:

We thank Thee, Almighty God, that through this gracious feast Thou hast refreshed and satisfied us, and we pray Thee that it may tend to the increase of our faith and to growth in godliness and all Christian virtues, through Thy Son, Jesus Christ, our Lord.

Or:

Lord Jesus Christ, Thou Who hast called us to this Holy Supper, we most heartily thank Thee for Thy mercy, that Thou hast nourished us with Thy Body and Blood, and that Thou hast filled and compassed us about with Thy goodness. O Lord, abide with us; into Thy hands we commit ourselves, and put our trust in Thee. Grant us to dwell with Thee forever.

The **Congregation** *shall sing:*

Advent, Christmas, and Epiphany Seasons.   Lenten Season.   Easter and Pentecost Seasons.   Trinity Season.

A - men.   A - men.   A - men.   A - men.

Advent, Christmas, and Epiphany Seasons.

The **Minister** *shall turn to the Congregation and sing or say:*

Preussische Kirchenordnung, 1525.

Let   us   thank   and   praise   the   Lord!

The **Congregation** *shall sing:*

Glo - ry   be   to   Thee,   O   Lord!   Hal - le-

lu - jah!   Hal - le - lu - jah!   Hal - le - lu - jah!

Lenten Season.

The **Minister:**

Let . . . us thank and praise the Lord!

The **Congregation:**

Nürnberger Agende, 1639.

Glo - ry   be   to

Thee,   O   Lord!   Hal-le-lu - jah!   Hal-le-lu - jah!   Hal-le-lu - jah!

Then shall the **Minister** *say:*

Bow your hearts to God, and receive the Benediction.

The Lord bless thee, and keep thee.   The Lord make His face shine upon thee, and be gracious unto thee.   The Lord lift up His countenance upon thee, and give thee peace.

In the Name of the Father, and of the Son, and of the Holy Spirit. Amen.

The **Minister** *shall turn to the Altar, and the* **Congregation** *shall sing:*

Advent, Christmas, and Epiphany Seasons.

A - men,   A - men,   A - - - - - men.

Lenten Season.

A - men,   A - men,   A - - - - men.

Easter and Pentecost Seasons.

A - men,   A - men,   A - - - - men.

Trinity Season.

A - men,   A - men,   A - - - - - men.

The Service shall close with silent prayer, while the **Congregation** *remains standing and the* **Minister** *kneels before the Altar.*

The Service

SECOND SETTING

¶ *The General Rubrics contain directions additional to those which appear in the Services.*
¶ *Intonations provided for the Minister's parts of the Services represent a permissive use. They are not to be considered directive.*
¶ *The preparatory office up to the Introit may be said. If it be sung, the following musical setting may be used.*

¶ *The Congregation shall rise. The Minister shall sing or say:*

 IN the Name of the Father, and of the Son, and of the Holy Ghost.

¶ *The Congregation shall sing or say:*

A - men.

THE CONFESSION OF SINS

¶ *The Minister shall say:*

BELOVED in the Lord! Let us draw near with a true heart, and confess our sins unto God our Father, beseeching him, in the Name of our Lord Jesus Christ, to grant us forgiveness.

¶ *The Minister and Congregation may kneel.*
¶ *They shall sing or say:*

Minister: Our help is in the Name of the Lord. ℟. Who made heaven and earth

Minister: I said, I will confess my transgressions unto the Lord. ℟. And thou forgavest the iniquity of my sin.

¶ *Then shall the Minister say:*

ALMIGHTY God, our Maker and Redeemer, we poor sinners confess unto thee, that we are by nature sinful and unclean, and that we have sinned against thee by thought, word, and deed. Wherefore we flee for refuge to thine infinite mercy, seeking and imploring thy grace, for the sake of our Lord Jesus Christ.

¶ *The Congregation shall say with the Minister:*

O MOST merciful God, who hast given thine only-begotten Son to die for us, have mercy upon us, and for his sake grant us remission of all our sins: and by thy Holy Spirit increase in us true knowledge of thee and of thy will, and true obedience to thy Word, that by thy grace we may come to everlasting life; through Jesus Christ our Lord. Amen.

¶ *Then the Minister, standing, and facing the Congregation, shall say:*

ALMIGHTY God, our heavenly Father, hath had mercy upon us, and hath given his only Son to die for us, and for his sake forgiveth us all our sins. To them that believe on his Name, he giveth power to become the sons of God, and bestoweth upon them his Holy Spirit. He that believeth, and is baptized, shall be saved. Grant this, O Lord, unto us all.

¶ *Or, he may say:*

THE Almighty and merciful God grant unto you, being penitent, pardon and remission of all your sins, time for amendment of life, and the grace and comfort of his Holy Spirit.

¶ *The Congregation shall sing or say:*

A - men.

¶ *A brief Silence may be kept before the Introit for the Day.*

¶ *The Congregation shall stand until the close of the Collect.*

INTROIT

¶ *The Introit for the Day with the Gloria Patri shall be sung or said. The Introit should be sung by the choir, or it may be said by the Minister.*

GLORIA PATRI

Plainsong, Tone V
PFALZ, 1557
Adapted, REGINA H. FRYXELL

Congregation. Unison

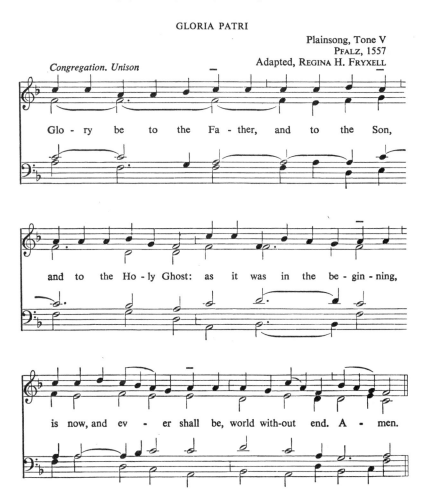

Glo - ry be to the Fa - ther, and to the Son,

and to the Ho - ly Ghost: as it was in the be - gin - ning,

is now, and ev - er shall be, world with-out end. A - men.

¶ *Then shall be sung or said the Kyrie.*

KYRIE

X cent. Plainsong (*Orbis factor*)
Swedish *Mässbok*, 1942
Adapted, REGINA H. FRYXELL

Congregation

R̷. Lord, - - - - - have mer - cy.

Minister

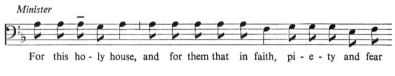

For this ho - ly house, and for them that in faith, pi - e - ty and fear

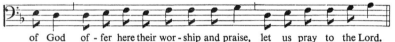

of God of - fer here their wor - ship and praise, let us pray to the Lord.

Congregation

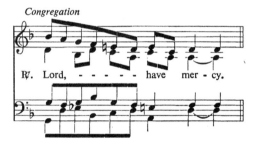

R̷. Lord, - - - - - have mer - cy.

Minister

Help, save, pi - ty and de - fend us, O God, by thy grace.

Congregation

R̷. A - - - men.

¶ In Lent the following Kyrie may be sung or said:

Bohemian Brethren, 1544
Swedish *Mässbok*, 1942
Adapted, REGINA H. FRYXELL

Minister

In peace let us pray to the Lord.

Congregation. Unison

R̃. Lord, - - - have mer - cy.

Minister

For the peace · that is from a - bove, and for the

sal - va - tion of our souls, let us pray to the Lord.

Congregation

R̃. Lord, - - - have mer - cy.

Minister

For the peace of the whole world, for the well - be - ing of the church-es

of God, and for the u - ni - ty of all, let us pray to the Lord.

Congregation

R̸. Lord, - - - have mer - cy.

Minister

For this ho - ly house, and for them that in faith, pi - e - ty and fear

of God of - fer here their wor-ship and praise, let us pray to the Lord.

Congregation

R̸. Lord, - - - have mer - cy.

Minister

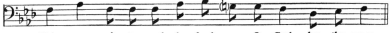

Help, save, pi - ty and de - fend us, O God, by thy grace.

Congregation

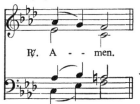

R̸. A - - men.

¶ In place of the foregoing, the following Kyrie may be sung or said:

KYRIE

Minister

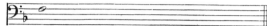

1. Lord, have mercy upon us.
2. Christ, have mercy upon us.
3. Lord, have mercy upon us.

Congregation

¶ *Then shall be sung or said the Gloria in Excelsis.*

GLORIA IN EXCELSIS

X cent. Plainsong (*Lux et origo*)
N. Decius, *Allein Gott in der Höh' sei Ehr*
Adapted, Regina H. Fryxell

Minister

Glo - - ry be to God on high!

Congregation. Unison

And on earth peace, good will toward men.

We praise thee, we bless thee, we wor-ship thee, we glo - ri - fy thee,

we give thanks to thee for thy great glo - ry, O Lord God,

heaven - ly King, God the Fa - ther Al - might - y.

O Lord, the on-ly be-got-ten Son, Je-sus Christ; O Lord God,

Lamb of God, Son of the Fa-ther, that tak-est a-way the

sin of the world, have mer-cy up-on us. Thou that tak-est a-

way the sin of the world, re-ceive our prayer. Thou that sit-test at the

right hand of God the Fa-ther, have mer-cy up-on us.

For thou on-ly art ho-ly; thou on-ly art the Lord;

thou on-ly, O Christ, with the Ho-ly Ghost, art most

high . . . . . in the glo-ry of God the Fa-ther. A-men.

Organ

¶ *Then shall the Minister sing or say:*

Congregation

The Lord be with you. ℟. And with thy spirit.

¶ *The Minister shall say:*

Let us pray.

¶ *Then shall the Minister say the Collect for the Day.*

THE COLLECT

¶ *The Collect ended, the Congregation shall sing or say:*

A - men.

¶ *Here the Minister may read the appointed Lesson from the Old Testament,* *saying:* The Lesson is written in the _____ Chapter of _____, beginning at the _____ Verse. *The Lesson ended, he shall say:* Here endeth the Lesson.

¶ *Then may be sung a Psalm or a hymn version of a Psalm.*

¶ *Then shall the Minister announce the Epistle for the Day, saying:* The Epistle for *(here he shall name the Festival or Day)* is written in the _____ Chapter of _____, beginning at the _____ Verse.

THE EPISTLE

¶ *The Epistle ended, the Minister shall say:* Here endeth the Epistle for the Day.

¶ *Then may the Gradual for the Day be sung.*

THE GRADUAL

¶ *When the Gradual for the Day is omitted, the Alleluia or the Gradual* *for the Season may be sung.*

THE ALLELUIA

Prussia, 1525
Based on X cent. Plainsong
Adapted, REGINA H. FRYXELL

Al - le - lu - ia,   Al - le - lu - ia,   Al - le - lu - - ia.

Or,

XI cent. Plainsong (*De angelis*)
Adapted, REGINA H. FRYXELL

Unison

Al - le - lu - ia, Al - le - lu - ia, Al - - - - le - lu - ia.

¶ *In Lent this Sentence shall be sung instead of the Alleluia:*

JOHN MERBECKE
Arr. HAROLD W. GILBERT

Unison

Christ hath hum - bled him - self, and be - come o -

be - dient un - to death: e - ven the death of the Cross.

¶ *Then shall the Minister announce the Gospel for the Day, saying:* The Holy Gospel
is written in the _____ Chapter of St. _____, beginning at the _____ Verse.

¶ *The Congregation shall rise and sing or say:*

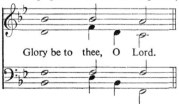

Glory be to thee, O Lord.

¶ *Then shall the Minister read the Gospel for the Day.*

THE GOSPEL

¶ *The Gospel ended, the Minister shall say:* Here endeth the Gospel for the Day.

¶ *The Congregation shall sing or say:*

Praise be to thee, O Christ.

¶ *Then shall be said or sung the Creed.*

THE CREED

¶ *The Nicene Creed shall be said or sung on all Festivals and whenever there is a Communion.*

THE NICENE CREED
I BELIEVE in one God, . . .

THE APOSTLES' CREED
I BELIEVE in God the Father Almighty, . . .

¶ *Then shall be sung the Hymn.*

THE HYMN

¶ *Then shall follow the Sermon.*

THE SERMON

¶ *The Sermon being ended, the Congregation shall rise and the Minister shall then say:*

THE peace of God, which passeth all understanding, keep your hearts and minds through Christ Jesus.

Congregation

A - men.

¶ *Then shall the Offering be received and presented at the Altar.*

THE OFFERING

¶ *Then shall follow the Offertory, the Congregation standing meanwhile. One of the Offertories here following, or any other suitable Offertory, shall be sung or said.*

¶ *When there is a Communion, the Minister, after Silent Prayer, and during the singing of the Offertory, shall uncover the Vessels and reverently prepare for the Administration of the Holy Sacrament.*

THE OFFERTORY
I

Litany in Phrygian Mode
Swedish *Mässbok*, 1942
Adapted, REGINA H. FRYXELL

The sac - ri - fic - es of God are a bro - ken spir - it:

a bro - ken and a con-trite heart, O God, thou wilt not de-spise.

Do good in thy good pleas-ure un - to Zi - on: build thou the

walls of Je - ru - sa - lem. Then shalt thou be pleased with the sac - ri -

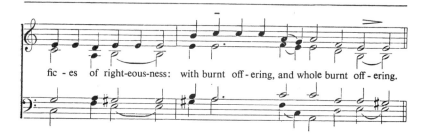

fic - es   of right-eous-ness: with burnt off - ering, and whole burnt off - ering.

II

For music of the second Offertory text, What shall I render unto the Lord . . . ,
see First Setting

III

Melody by J. G. WINER
Adapted, REGINA H. FRYXELL

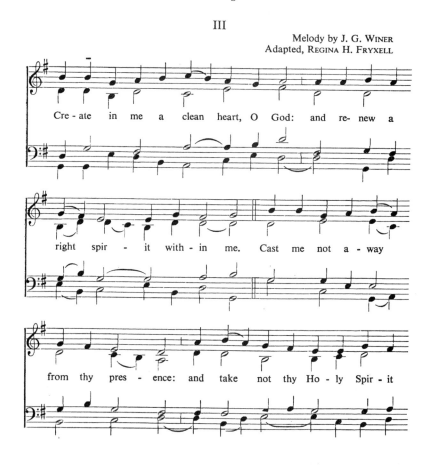

Cre - ate   in   me   a   clean   heart, O   God: and re- new   a

right   spir - it   with - in   me.   Cast   me   not   a - way

from   thy   pres - ence: and   take   not   thy   Ho - ly   Spir - it

from me. Re - store un - to me the joy of thy sal -

va - tion: and up - hold me with thy free Spir - it.

¶ *Then shall follow the Prayer of the Church.*

THE PRAYER OF THE CHURCH

Let us pray.

ALMIGHTY God, the Father of our Lord Jesus Christ . . .

¶ *If there be no Communion the Minister and Congregation shall say the Lord's Prayer.*

OUR Father, who art in heaven, . . .

¶ *A Hymn may then be sung. Then the Minister, standing at the Altar, shall sing or say the Benediction.*

THE BENEDICTION

THE LORD bless thee, and keep thee.
The LORD make his face shine upon thee, and
be gracious unto thee.
The LORD lift up his countenance upon thee, and
give thee peace:
In the Name of the Father, and of the Son, and of the
Holy Ghost.

¶ *The Congregation shall sing or say:*

For music, see p. 144   Amen.

THE THANKSGIVING

¶ *A Hymn shall be sung.*
¶ *The Congregation shall rise at the beginning of the Preface.*

THE PREFACE

¶ *The Minister and Congregation shall sing or say:*

The LORD be with you

R̹. And with thy spir - it.

Lift up your hearts.

R̹. We lift them up un - to the Lord.

Let us give thanks un - to the Lord our God.

R̹. It is meet and right so to do.

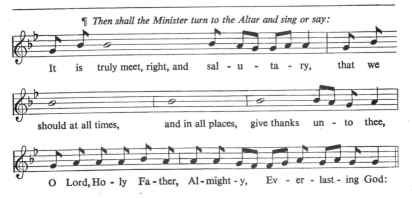

¶ Then shall the Minister turn to the Altar and sing or say:

It is truly meet, right, and sal-u-ta-ry, that we should at all times, and in all places, give thanks un-to thee, O Lord, Ho-ly Fa-ther, Al-might-y, Ev-er-last-ing God:

¶ Here shall follow the Proper Preface for the Day or Season. If there be none especially appointed, then shall follow immediately, Therefore with Angels, etc.
¶ For music of the Proper Prefaces, see pp. 71-74, Service Book and Hymnal.

PROPER PREFACES

For Advent

WHO didst comfort thy people with the promise of the Redeemer, through whom thou wilt also make all things new in the day when he shall come again to judge the world in righteousness. Therefore with Angels, *etc.*

For Christmas

FOR in the mystery of the Word made flesh, thou hast given us a new revelation of thy glory; that seeing thee in the person of thy Son, we may be drawn to the love of those things which are not seen. Therefore with Angels, *etc.*

For Epiphany

AND now do we praise thee, that thou didst send unto us thine only-begotten Son, and that in him, being found in fashion as a man, thou didst reveal the fullness of thy glory. Therefore with Angels, *etc.*

For Lent

WHO on the Tree of the Cross didst give salvation unto mankind; that whence death arose, thence life also might rise again: and that he who by a tree once overcame, might likewise by a Tree be overcome, through Christ our Lord: through whom with Angels, *etc.*

For Easter

BUT chiefly are we bound to praise thee for the glorious Resurrection of thy Son, Jesus Christ our Lord: for he is the very Paschal Lamb, which was offered for us, and hath taken away the sin of the world; who by his death hath destroyed death, and by his rising to life again hath restored to us everlasting life. Therefore with Angels, *etc.*

For the Ascension of our Lord

THROUGH Jesus Christ our Lord, who, after his Resurrection, appeared openly to all his disciples, and in their sight was taken up into heaven, that he might make us partakers of his divine Nature. Therefore with Angels, *etc.*

For the Day of Pentecost

THROUGH Jesus Christ our Lord, who, ascending above the heavens and sitting at thy right hand, poured out on this day the Holy Spirit, as he had promised, upon the chosen disciples; whereat the whole earth rejoices with exceeding joy. Therefore with Angels, *etc.*

For Trinity Sunday

WHO with thine only-begotten Son, and the Holy Ghost, art one God, one Lord. And in the confession of the only true God, we worship the Trinity in Person, and the Unity in Substance, of Majesty co-equal. Therefore with Angels, *etc.*

For All Saints' Day (or at any time when the faithful departed are remembered)

THROUGH Jesus Christ our Lord, who in the blessedness of thy saints hath given us a glorious pledge of the hope of our calling; that, following their example and being strengthened by their fellowship, we may exult in thee for thy mercy, even as they rejoice with thee in glory. Therefore with Angels, *etc.*

¶ *After the Preface shall follow immediately:*

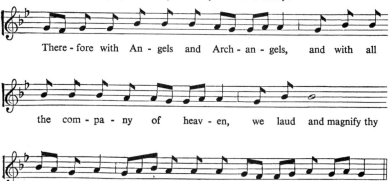

There - fore with An - gels and Arch - an - gels, and with all the com - pa - ny of heav - en, we laud and magnify thy glo - rious Name; ev - er - more prais - ing thee, and say - ing:

¶ Then shall be sung or said the Sanctus.

THE SANCTUS

X cent. Plainsong
Swedish *Mässbok*, 1942
Adapted, REGINA H. FRYXELL

Slowly, in unison

Ho - ly, ho - - - ly, ho - - ly, Lord God of Sa - ba - oth;

Heav - en and earth are full of thy glo - ry; Ho -

san - na in the high - est. Bless - ed is he that com - eth

in the Name of the Lord; Ho - san - na in the high - est.

¶ *Then may the Congregation kneel.*

¶ *The Minister standing before the Altar, and facing it, shall say the Prayer of Thanksgiving.*

THE PRAYER OF THANKSGIVING

HOLY art thou, Almighty and Merciful God. Holy art thou, and great is the Majesty of thy glory.

Thou didst so love the world as to give thine only-begotten Son, that whosoever believeth in him might not perish, but have everlasting life; Who, having come into the world to fulfill for us thy holy will and to accomplish all things for our salvation, IN THE NIGHT IN WHICH HE WAS BETRAYED, ªTOOK BREAD; AND, WHEN HE HAD GIVEN THANKS, HE BRAKE IT AND GAVE IT TO HIS DISCIPLES, SAYING, TAKE, EAT; THIS IS MY BODY, WHICH IS GIVEN FOR YOU; THIS DO IN REMEMBRANCE OF ME.

(a) Here he shall take the BREAD *in his hand.*

AFTER THE SAME MANNER ALSO, HE ᵇTOOK THE CUP, WHEN HE HAD SUPPED, AND, WHEN HE HAD GIVEN THANKS, HE GAVE IT TO THEM, SAYING, DRINK YE ALL OF IT; THIS CUP IS THE NEW TESTAMENT IN MY BLOOD, WHICH IS SHED FOR YOU, AND FOR MANY, FOR THE REMISSION OF SINS; THIS DO, AS OFT AS YE DRINK IT, IN REMEMBRANCE OF ME.

(b) Here he shall take the CUP *in his hand.*

Remembering, therefore, his salutary precept, his life-giving Passion and Death, his glorious Resurrection and Ascension and the promise of his coming again, we give thanks to thee, O Lord God Almighty, not as we ought, but as we are able; and we beseech thee mercifully to accept our praise and thanksgiving, and with thy Word and Holy Spirit to bless us, thy servants, and these thine own gifts of bread and wine, so that we and all who partake thereof may be filled with heavenly benediction and grace, and, receiving the remission of sins, be sanctified in soul and body, and have our portion with all thy saints.

And unto thee, O God, Father, Son, and Holy Spirit, be all honor and glory in thy holy Church, world without end. Amen.

¶ *Then shall the Minister sing or say:*

OUR Father, who art in heaven, Hallowed be thy Name, Thy kingdom come, Thy will be done, on earth as it is in heaven. Give us this day our daily bread; And forgive us our trespasses, as we forgive those who trespass against us; And lead us not into temptation, But deliver us from evil.

¶ *The Congregation shall sing or say:*

Ancient Church Melody
Harm. by WINFRED DOUGLAS

For thine is the king - dom, and the power, and the

glo - ry, for - ev - er and ev - er. A - men.

¶ *Or, instead of the above Prayer of Thanksgiving,* "Holy art thou, Almighty and Merciful God," *the Minister may say the Words of Institution, followed by the Lord's Prayer.*

THE WORDS OF INSTITUTION

OUR LORD JESUS CHRIST, IN THE NIGHT IN WHICH HE WAS BETRAYED, [a]TOOK BREAD; AND, WHEN HE HAD GIVEN THANKS, HE BRAKE IT AND GAVE IT TO HIS DISCIPLES, SAYING, TAKE, EAT; THIS IS MY BODY, WHICH IS GIVEN FOR YOU; THIS DO IN REMEMBRANCE OF ME.

(a) *Here he shall take the* BREAD *in his hand.*

AFTER THE SAME MANNER ALSO, HE [b]TOOK THE CUP, WHEN HE HAD SUPPED, AND, WHEN HE HAD GIVEN THANKS, HE GAVE IT TO THEM, SAYING, DRINK YE ALL OF IT; THIS CUP IS THE NEW TESTAMENT IN MY BLOOD, WHICH IS SHED FOR YOU, AND FOR MANY, FOR THE REMISSION OF SINS; THIS DO, AS OFT AS YE DRINK IT, IN REMEMBRANCE OF ME.

(b) *Here he shall take the* CUP *in his hand.*

THE LORD'S PRAYER

OUR Father, who art in heaven, . . . Amen.

¶ *Then shall the Minister turn to the Congregation and sing or say:*

The peace of the Lord be with you al - way.

¶ *The Congregation shall sing or say:*

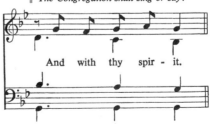

And with thy spir - it.

¶ *Then, the Congregation standing, shall be sung or said the Agnus Dei.*

AGNUS DEI

BRAUNSCHWEIG, 1528
Adapted, REGINA H. FRYXELL

O Christ, thou Lamb of God, that tak-est a-way the sin of the world, have mer-cy up-on us. O Christ, thou Lamb of God, that tak-est a-way the sin of the world, have mer-cy up-on us. O Christ, thou Lamb of God, that tak-est a-way the sin

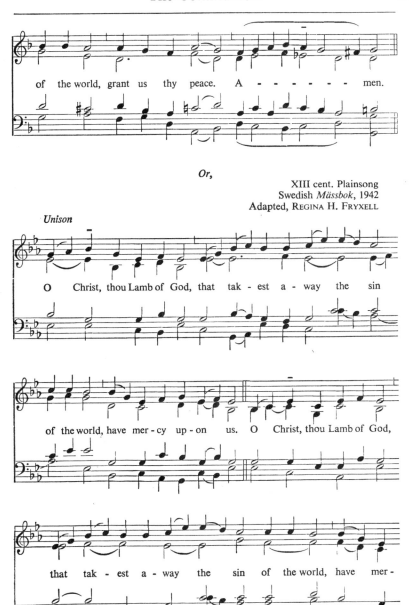

of the world, grant us thy peace. A - - - - - - men.

Or,

XIII cent. Plainsong
Swedish *Mässbok*, 1942
Adapted, REGINA H. FRYXELL

Unison

O Christ, thou Lamb of God, that tak - est a - way the sin

of the world, have mer - cy up - on us. O Christ, thou Lamb of God,

that tak - est a - way the sin of the world, have mer -

cy up - on us. O Christ, thou Lamb of God, that tak - est

a - way the sin of the world, grant us thy peace. A - men.

*¶ Then shall the Communicants present themselves before the Altar
and receive the Holy Sacrament.*

THE COMMUNION

¶ When the Minister giveth the BREAD he shall say:

The Body of Christ, given for thee.

¶ When he giveth the CUP he shall say:

The Blood of Christ, shed for thee.

¶ The Communicant may say Amen after each Element has been received.

*¶ After he hath given the BREAD and the CUP, or after all have been communicated, the
Minister shall say:*

The Body of our Lord Jesus Christ and his precious Blood strengthen and
preserve you unto eternal life.

THE POST-COMMUNION

¶ Then shall the Congregation rise, and the Nunc Dimittis may be sung or said:

NUNC DIMITTIS

Plainsong, Tone V
SOEST, 1532; PFALZ, 1557
Adapted, REGINA H. FRYXELL

Lord, now let - test thou thy ser - vant de - part in peace:

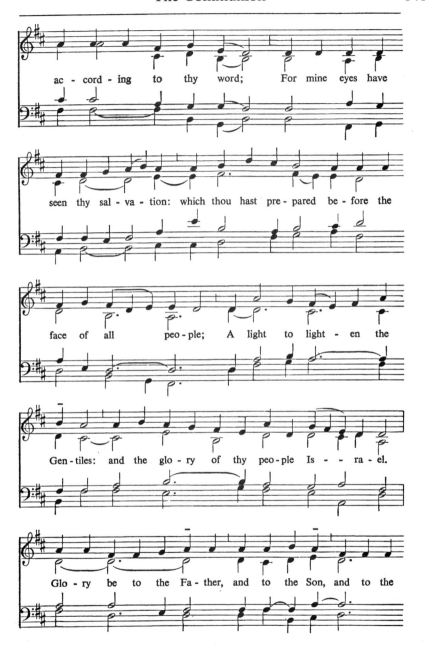

Ho - ly Ghost: As it was in the be - gin - ning, is now, and

ev - - - er shall be, world with - out end. A - men.

¶ *Then shall be said The Prayer.*

THE PRAYER

¶ *The Minister shall say one of the following Prayers; or he may say the Collect
for Thursday in Holy Week.*

Minister   Congregation

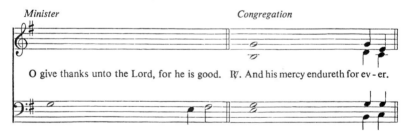

O give thanks unto the Lord, for he is good. ℟. And his mercy endureth for ev - er.

WE give thanks to thee, Almighty God, that thou hast refreshed us with
this thy salutary gift; and we beseech thee, of thy mercy, to strengthen
us through the same gift, in faith toward thee and in fervent love toward one
another; through Jesus Christ, thy dear Son, our Lord, who liveth and reigneth with thee and the Holy Ghost, one God, world without end.

Or,

POUR forth upon us, O Lord, the spirit of thy love, that by thy mercy thou mayest make of one will those whom thou hast fed with one heavenly food; through thy Son, Jesus Christ our Lord, who liveth and reigneth with thee and the Holy Ghost, one God, world without end.

Or,

ALMIGHTY God, who givest the true Bread which cometh down from heaven, even thy Son, Jesus Christ our Lord: Grant, we beseech thee, that we who have received the Sacrament of his Body and Blood may abide in him, and he in us, that we may be filled with the power of his endless life; who liveth and reigneth with thee and the Holy Ghost, one God, world without end.

Or,

ALMIGHTY God, who hast given thine only Son to be unto us both a sacrifice for sin and also an ensample of godly life: Give us grace that we may always most thankfully receive that his inestimable benefit, and also daily endeavor ourselves to follow the blessed steps of his most holy life; through the same Jesus Christ our Lord, who liveth and reigneth with thee and the Holy Ghost, one God, world without end.

¶ *The Congregation shall sing or say:*

A - men.

¶ *Then may be sung or said the Salutation and the Benedicamus.*

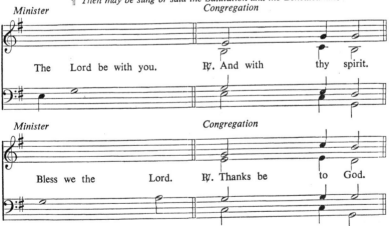

Minister — The Lord be with you. ℟. And with thy spirit.

Minister — Bless we the Lord. ℟. Thanks be to God.

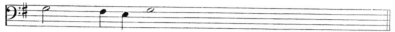

¶ Then the Minister, standing at the Altar, shall sing or say the Benediction.

THE BENEDICTION

Minister

THE LORD bless thee, and keep thee.
The LORD make his face shine upon thee, and be gracious unto thee.

The LORD lift up his countenance upon thee, and give thee peace:

In the Name of the Father, and of the Son, and of the Holy Ghost.

¶ The Congregation shall sing or say:

A - men.   *Or,*   A - - men.

Or,

A - men, A - men, A - - - men.

Or,

A - men, A - men, A - - men.

First Lines of Hymns

146